The Road Back to
SANITY

Finding Our Way Home from Cultural Delusion

FRANK WRIGHT, PH.D.

D. JAMES
KENNEDY
MINISTRIES

THE ROAD BACK TO SANITY
Finding Our Way Home from Cultural Delusion

By Frank Wright, Ph.D.

ISBN: 978-1-929626-70-0

Cover and Interior Design: Roark Creative, www.roarkcreative.com

Printed in the United States of America.

Published by:

D. James Kennedy Ministries
P.P.O. Box 11786
Fort Lauderdale, FL 33339
1-800-988-7884
www.DJamesKennedyMinistries.org
letters@djameskennedy.org

Dedication

To Anne Kennedy, a sweet southern gal
who grew to be a cherished daughter, a loving wife and
mother, a faithful friend to many, and a devoted servant of her
dear Savior. Your beauty still shines through the years.

CONTENTS

FOREWORD

There is a cycle of nations seen in the Old Testament book of Judges. When Israel went into the Promised Land making a covenant with God, Israel was blessed, but afterward began to worship the gods of other nations. God sent prophets calling Israel to repent. Usually they did not repent—until God brought judgment, letting them be overrun by their historic enemies. In their suffering Israel eventually did cry out in repentance, and in His mercy God sent a deliverer, like Gideon, Samson, Deborah, and others.

Sadly, while the renewal of their covenant with God brought renewed blessings, in their prosperity they once again forgot God and their backsliding began anew. We see this cycle thirteen times in the book of Judges: covenant renewal, followed by blessing, followed by backsliding, followed by the visitation of prophets, followed by the judgment of God, followed by repentance and the provision of a deliverer.

This cycle has important implications for America because in a very real way America also made a covenant with God. In the Declaration of Independence the signers make the bold claim that they are "appealing to the Supreme Judge of the world for the rectitude of our intentions." And with that appeal of faith America was blessed with independence.

America's national blessing continued in ways great and small—with Eli Whitney inventing the cotton gin, with Robert Fulton inventing the steamboat, and with Samuel Morse inventing the telegraph, and so on. America eventually became the most prosperous nation on earth, yet it did not honor the rectitude of its intentions, failing to rid the land of the blight of slavery—and one people prospered from the unrequited sweat and blood of others. "Prophets" came calling for national repentance—the abolitionists. But we did not repent. And judgment came, with more than a half million people dying in the subsequent Civil War.

In the middle of that war Abraham Lincoln, with all his faults, called the nation to repent with his *Proclamation Appointing a National Fast Day.* By and large, the nation did repent and subsequently renewed its covenant with God by dedicating an annual day of thanksgiving and deciding to put "In God We Trust" on our national coin. Since then we have repeated the cycle of blessing and judgment to major and minor degrees.

In his Second Inaugural Address President Lincoln spoke of national judgment possibly continuing:

> *. . . until every drop of blood drawn with the lash shall be paid by another drawn with the sword, as was said three thousand years ago, so still it must be said "the judgments of the Lord are true and righteous altogether."*

Surely in our day also we are inviting judgment. We see the destruction of the innocent unborn on an unparalleled scale. We see governments kicking God out of the schools. We see the redefinition of marriage and a rapidly emerging cultural hostility to the Bible and historic Christianity. And now we see unprecedented threats to our national security. One cannot help but wonder: Is anyone going to connect the dots? Are we again a nation that has abandoned and forgotten the God who gave us life?

With our need for national repentance so pressing, and the need for America to return to the paths of blessing trod by our forebears, I am pleased to see this book by Dr. Frank Wright, *The Road Back to Sanity: Finding Our Way Home from Cultural Delusion.* I recommend this book as a powerful reminder that God has not given us a spirit of fear. Now is the time for Christians to step up and faithfully proclaim the Gospel—and to engage the culture with the mind of Christ.

William J. Federer
Author of *America's God & Country Quotations*

INTRODUCTION

When you don't know where you are going, any road will take you there.

(A paraphrase of the Cheshire Cat speaking to Alice)

A professor walks into a college classroom carrying a large glass beaker, a pitcher of water, and a large paper grocery bag. She smiles at the class and silently places the glass beaker on the desk.

Reaching into the grocery bag she takes out a collection of large rocks and begins filling the beaker. When she can no longer get any more rocks into the beaker, she turns to the class and asks: "Is the glass full?" They reply in the affirmative.

The professor then pulls a smaller bag of pea-sized gravel out of the grocery bag, shaking its contents into the beaker, so that the gravel fills the spaces around the large rocks. She turns to the class again and says: "Is the glass full?" The room now is full of hesitation, with only a smattering of positive responses.

Next out of the large grocery bag comes a smaller bag of sand, which the professor pours into the beaker shaking it until the sand settles into the spaces around the large rocks and gravel. "Is the glass full?" The students are now united in the negative.

Finally our creative pedagogue takes the water pitcher in hand and fills the beaker to the brim. "Is the glass now full? With the admission that the beaker finally is full, all eyes are on the professor who turns to the class and says: "What was the point of this demonstration?"

Most student responses are a variant of a time-management theme, implying that a well-organized life is necessary to accomplish much of anything.

With a broad smile on her face, the professor declaims in a firm but encouraging tone: "The solitary point I wish to make is this: If you do not put the large rocks in first, you will never get them in at all."

PRIORITIES AND UNINTENDED CONSEQUENCES

Our clever instructor memorably highlights an important life principle: a meaningful and productive life (at least in part) is about identifying what matters most and dealing with those things first. But life is far more than setting priorities. In our day we have a failure even to understand which rocks matter most and why.

Part of our problem is a failure to recognize that some issues (rocks) constitute threshold matters that once decided, have a far-reaching impact in ways difficult to comprehend before crossing the threshold. This is sometimes called the Law of Unintended Consequences.

Well known in the school of social sciences,[1] the Law of Unintended Consequences describes outcomes that were not foreseen or intended by some premeditated action. These unanticipated results tend to be grouped in three classes:

1. Outcomes with an unexpected serendipitous benefit
2. Outcomes with an unexpected detrimental drawback
3. Outcomes with a perverse result contrary to the one intended.

An example of a perverse and unintended result would be the rise of bacteria that are highly resistant to traditional antibiotics, which emerges as a consequence of the widespread and beneficial use of these same antibiotics. Antibiotics in general are enormously beneficial to human and animal health. The increasing appearance of these super-resistant strains of bacteria, however, poses a substantial and alarming threat—one that many researchers argue can be traced to the overuse of antibiotics.[2]

We find another example of The Law of Unintended Consequences at work in welfare policy. In 1964, President Lyndon Johnson declared the so-called War on Poverty. For a reference point, note that in 1960, the rate of births to unmarried mothers was 5 percent.[3]

Over the next few decades, welfare programs expanded

dramatically, with most assistance being "means-tested." The means-testing component seemed perfectly logical at the time. Those with lesser means received more assistance. This approach, however, unwittingly penalized marriage. A single mother received far less assistance if she married the father of her children—10 to 20 percent less.

Fast forward to 2014, when the rate of births to unwed mothers is 40 percent (29 percent among whites, 53 percent among Hispanics, and 70 percent among blacks). In the most perverse result imaginable, welfare policies initiated and expanded in the War on Poverty ended up incentivizing the very behaviors most likely to perpetuate poverty.[4]

Sadly, examples of the Law of Unintended Consequences are legion, with perverse results contrary to the one intended becoming increasingly evident over time. One cannot help wondering what might be the unintended consequences and perverse outcomes of the Supreme Court's ruling on same sex marriage.

Economist Henry Hazlitt argues that these perverse outcomes flow from fallacious reasoning driven by two key factors: 1) antagonistic self-interest; and 2) the failure to account for secondary consequences.[5] When we fail to account for these factors, the road ahead will be continually pockmarked by perverse outcomes—most of them unintended.

FOUR CULTURAL BYWAYS TO DELUSION

If you are like me, you look around and see a world seemingly gone insane. In two generations, we have witnessed unparalleled destruction of preborn children, the systematic demolition of the family, a rampantly sexualized culture epitomizing the word pagan, and a tyrannical redefinition of marriage.

This brief volume will examine four roadways of our cultural journey where the rule and reign of antagonistic self-interest and the Law of Unintended Consequences are especially acute. If left unchecked, our passage along these byways may lead to shadowy twilight years, and even to bondage. But if we can better understand these misbegotten byways, it may not be too late to regain our bearings and get back on course in defense of freedom, so that an unfettered Gospel can be proclaimed here and around the world.

Separation of Church and State

The collapse of a rational understanding (either philosophical or theological) of separation of church and state is the gateway to tyranny. Sound like too much? Well, history is not silent on this subject. While it is true that historical concerns over religion having a dominating influence in government are not without foundation, the overwhelming lesson of history rather is that systematic government domination of religion is the more well-established norm. America was born into the community of nations because devout followers of Christ fled the unending assault by government upon the church. Wisely, our own First Amendment was designed to protect against both problems through the Establishment Clause and the Free Exercise Clause. Nevertheless, the historical pattern holds, as government (especially socialist) violations of the Free Exercise Clause in our day are inarguable, while by contrast expressed concerns over violations of the Establishment Clause seem to range from the chimerical to the comical.

Executive Overreach

Perhaps the clearest foreshadowing of totalitarian socialism is methodical and unswerving executive overreach. This is so because power attained is never enough and is followed by a continual grasping for more. The Founders of the American republic knew this well; hence the Constitution's clearly articulated doctrine of the separation of powers. In 18th century France, Louis XIV is reputed to have said: *L'etat, c'est moi* (I am the state). No political leader in their right mind would say such a thing today, but some seem to behave as if it were so. Of particular concern are executive orders that usurp the authority of other branches of government. The end-justifies-the-means rationale of such executive actions has more in common with Mao and Mussolini than with Locke and Burke.

Socialism

Many people (less so among the young) know socialism to be an economic, political, and military system that has failed spectacularly wherever it has been tried. President Ronald Reagan called it a form of insanity.[6] Less well known is that socialism is the prototypical summation of rebellion against the authority of God. In fact, even as matter finds its antithesis in antimatter, legitimate human government (as delegated by God) is mirrored antithetically in socialism. Socialism will brook no compromise with any competing authority. All authority belongs to the state, and its citizens have but one duty: submission.

Gender Identity

Long a topic of bewilderment for many, gender identity is a cultural singularity that in many respects embodies each of the three issues preceding it. By systematically creating a silent public square, devoid of religious influence, the *de facto* "religion" becomes the secular creed of "choice." In the case of gender identity it is a choice marked by brokenness, dysphoria, and depression, separated from biological reality.

With the advent of systemic executive overreach, historic notions of tolerance are swept away, replaced by a fascistic notion that demands celebration, not mere acceptance. Failure to celebrate will have you branded a "hater." The re-education camps await only the consolidation of power necessary to implement them—likely without benefit or bother of any statutory support.

With the advent of full-orbed socialism, gender identity will become the religion of the secular state. And as the law of God will always stand in opposition to the authority of the secular state, religion (principally the Christian religion) will bow before the high priests of civic secularism or be swept away—all in the name of social justice.

THE COMMONALITY OF THESE ISSUES

Before we commence our survey of these threshold issues, worth noting is the insidious harmony between and among them. Each seems woven from the same frayed, discolored cultural fabric, in that:

1. Each overturns multiplied generations of reasoned experience and commonsense;

2. Each represents a morphing from rational thought to ideological self-interest;

3. Each draws breath from the winds of political correctness now run amuck;

4. Each advances by tyrannical power politics, overthrowing "we the people"; and

5. Each is a blatant rebellion against God's design and authority.

> ## The object of life is not to be on the side of the majority, but to escape finding oneself in the ranks of the insane.[7]

(Marcus Aurelius, philosopher, Roman emperor)

CHAPTER ONE

THE SILENT PUBLIC SQUARE
The Insanity of Attempts to Separate God from the State

Modern politics is civil war
carried on by other means.[8]

(Alasdair MacIntyre)

The fundamental basis of this nation's
laws was given to Moses on the Mount
... If we don't have a proper fundamental
moral background, we will finally end
up with a totalitarian government which
does not believe in rights for anybody
except the State.[9]

(Harry S. Truman)

He answered them: "I tell you, if these
should be silent, the stones would
immediately cry out."

(Luke 19:40)

Supreme Court Justice Oliver Wendell Holmes reportedly said there were "phrases that serve as an excuse for not thinking." In our time, surely the "separation of church and state" is one of those phrases. Perhaps nowhere is the cultural roadway to delusion more evident than in our contemporary preponderance to willfully misinterpret the principle of the separation of church and state.

After 158 years of largely settled First Amendment jurisprudence, our modern separationist insanity first reared its ugly head less than 70 years ago. In these latter days, arguments about it are generally detached from the original understanding and intent of those who ratified the Constitution. These arguments often have the additional charm of being incomplete, illogical, deceptive, and divisive. And those are their good qualities.

Along with the division and deception, we see everywhere the Straw Man in his tattered garments, arguing that a ten-year old with a Bible will bring down the republic, and charming those whose capacity for critical reasoning is less than robust. Also, everywhere we find the socialist establishmentarians[10] using this perverted doctrine in an attempt to drive every vestige of religion from the public square. Which is to say that the real aim of contemporary proponents of the separation of church and state is the Silent Public Square—one devoid of religious expression.

WHAT'S WRONG WITH SEPARATION?

What's really wrong with the separation of church and state, you say? Well, nothing and everything. Nothing is wrong with it, if rightly understood. But almost everything is wrong with the way it has been redefined and vehemently and asymmetrically applied today.

The Marketplace is Closed

We live in a time where the "marketplace of ideas" is wide open for all opinions—all opinions, that is, except Christian viewpoints in general, and the Bible in particular. According to D. James Kennedy and Jerry Newcombe, this state of affairs flows from a misunderstanding of the classical idea of the separation of church and state:

> *This misunderstanding has become a powerful hammer pounding away at the public expression of Christianity.*[11]

This "powerful hammer" is the *modus operandi* of our friends at the American Civil Liberties Union (ACLU), who regularly can be found in the forefront of the battle to suppress religious speech in the name of separation of church and state. While we can sometimes commend the ACLU for their zeal in defending unpopular speech, they are generally even quicker to snatch away the religious free speech rights of little schoolchildren in the name of separation of church and state.

This manly defense of the so-called wall of separation (which seems unaccountably threatened by a ten-year old with a Bible) is generally done with extortion-like demand letters in which the ACLU will threaten (with fine-sounding words, mind you) the local school board with millions of dollars in legal fees if they refuse to capitulate. Without help, they usually do.[12]

Here I must confess to an unseemly bit of *schadenfreude*,[13] as I recently observed the ACLU having difficulty with one of its workers' unions. It seems the ACLU president complained to the *Village Voice* that the union was using "a subtle form of extortion" by criticizing the ACLU to the press.[14] Ah yes, "the pot calling the kettle black," as my dad would say.[15]

In examining the insanity of using the separation of church and state as a means to drive religion from the public square, let's first review some important concepts that will enable us to tighten our focus on the heart of the matter—which is the so-called Establishment Clause of the First Amendment.

SOME THRESHOLD CONCEPTS

Restrictions Upon Whom?

In trying to grasp the error of contemporary jurisprudence on separation of church and state, let's begin with some threshold and essential ideas. First up is the First Amendment itself:

> *Congress shall make no law respecting an establishment of religion, or prohibiting the free exercise thereof; or abridging the freedom of speech, or of the press; or the right of the people to peaceably assemble, and to petition the government for the redress of grievances.*[16]

For our purposes the five most critical words in this amendment are: "Congress shall make no law." The clear but often overlooked point being that the first ten amendments to the Constitution—what we call the Bill of Rights—are all restrictions of the powers of *the federal government*. Did you get that? In the creation of this new central government, the framers of the Constitution feared the day when the minnow would become a whale. And that leviathan needed to be restrained from the outset. The Bill of Rights embodies freedoms as well as those restraints.

Note the five components of the First Amendment: 1) freedom of religion; 2) freedom of speech; 3) freedom of the press; 4) freedom of assembly; and 5) the freedom to petition the government for a redress of grievances. While these are easily understood—the framers of the Constitution certainly intended them so—they are not without limitation.

Freedom of speech for example is not without boundaries. One has no free-speech right to shout "fire" in a crowded theater because of the potential threat to the health and safety of others. Nor can one commit treason by communicating national security secrets to foreign powers and afterward claim free speech protection.

The same goes for things like libel, slander, child pornography, obscenity, etc. There always are boundaries to freedom. Personal freedom without boundaries goes by other names: anarchy and chaos. These boundaries are true of the freedom of religion also. If you form a church and your "god" teaches that you should overthrow all human government, good luck with that. Churches are a part of civil society. The question is: What should that civil society look like?

The First Freedom

In this discussion it is critically important that we recognize which of the five freedoms detailed in the First Amendment is listed first. This is called the Ordinal Question—which one goes first, second, and so on? This is a matter of no small importance, as we will see.

The first right specified in the First Amendment is, of course, religious freedom. We call it the First Freedom for this very reason. When the architects of the Constitution designed the Bill of Rights, they started first with the freedom upon which all others rested. Without religious freedom, free speech protections are chimerical. Without religious freedom, the freedom of assembly is illusory. Without religious freedom, the marketplace of ideas is closed and the freedom of press is of no account. Without religious freedom, a petition for redress of grievances is received with the sound of one hand clapping.

And as it relates to religious freedom, the Bill of Rights put constraints on the federal government—not on the church. "Congress shall make no law . . ."

Two Religion Clauses

Freedom of religion is, indeed, America's First Freedom. It is expressed in two distinct components—two clauses that make up one sentence in the stated freedom:

> *1) Congress shall make no law respecting an estab-lishment of religion, 2) or prohibiting the free exercise thereof...*

For clarity we might write it this way:

> *Congress shall make no law respecting an **establish-ment** of religion; and Congress shall make no law prohibiting the **free exercise** of religion.*

From this we get the familiar legal references to the *Establishment Clause* and/or the *Free Exercise Clause.* The distinction is important because of their unique purposes in the landscape of religious freedom.

THE ESTABLISHMENT CLAUSE RIGHTLY UNDERSTOOD

Even a broad-brush review of history reveals the original intent of the framers of the Constitution with respect to religious establishment—they did not want it at the federal level. No established national church. But that does not mean the idea of establishment was universally opposed. In fact at the time of the American Revolution, 9 of the 13 original colonies had established state churches.

Yet a federally established church would have been anathema and in direct conflict with the practices of a majority of the states—the very states expected to ratify the Constitution. But why was it anathematized? What were the attributes of religious establishment that were so problematic at the founding?

Michael McConnell's excellent legal survey of religious establishment in the founding era highlights some surprising attitudes and understandings of the founding generation, as well as the essential observable elements of a genuine religious establishment.[17] For example, McConnell says:

> *Unlike many modern Americans, most members of the founding generation believed deeply that some type of religious conviction was necessary for public virtue, and hence republican government.*[18]

Furthermore, McConnell argues that it is historically self-evident that:

> *When the words "Congress shall make no law respecting an establishment of religion" were added to the Constitution, virtually every American—and certainly every educated lawyer or statesman—knew from experience what those words meant.*[19]

This was so because, while 9 of the 13 original colonies had government-established churches, even after the adoption of the First Amendment half of the states continued to have some form of established religion. Many other Americans had some experience with or knowledge of established churches on the European continent.

And here is an important point:

> **Established churches were a widely familiar institution before and after the ratification of the Constitution with its seminal Establishment Clause in the First Amendment.**

The Key Elements of Establishment

So Americans were well versed in the pros and cons of the establishment of religion. But what did that look like? What are the distinctive elements of authentic religious establishment?

In its simplest and most basic form, an establishment is "the promotion of a common set of beliefs through governmental authority."[20] The laws enacting established religions varied widely across the colonies, but six attributes were generally evident.

1. Government control of the doctrine, structure, and personnel of the state church

This included government control of the content of the liturgy and other elements of worship. In the Church of England (which five colonies had as their established church) the doctrines, and liturgy of the church were determined by an act of Parliament. In the other colonies the individual assemblies exercised control over the articles of faith for their state churches.

In Washington, D.C., the expression "personnel is policy" illustrates the importance of having the right people in place to control the policies being advanced. In the same way, the colonial power to appoint (and remove) bishops and other clergy is the ultimate form of control by government.[21] And government certainly controlled the established state churches.

2. Mandatory attendance at religious worship services in the state church

Colonial legislatures enacted laws compelling attendance in the state church, accompanied by significant penalties for failure to do so. Attendance at other denominational churches was later deemed acceptable.[22] Here the power to require a man or woman's physical presence exemplifies the most powerful form of control a government can exert over an individual.

3. Public financial support

In England the land holdings of the churches were their means of financial support. In the colonies, financial support came from land grants and also from mandatory taxes (often called tithes) levied to support churches and ministers.

4. Prohibition of religious worship in other denominations

Restricting public religious worship to the established church was a common practice throughout Western Europe. Some of this flowed from the Protestant-Roman Catholic divide—a breach evident throughout the colonies. These same kinds of worship restrictions were common in the colonies themselves.

Enforcement of these prohibitions often looked like persecution, which moved James Madison to express passion and frustration in a letter to a college friend:

> *That diabolical, hell-conceived principle of persecution rages among some . . . There are at this time in the adjacent county not less than five or six well-meaning men in close jail, for publishing their religious sentiments, which in the main are very orthodox . . . I have squabbled and scolded, abused and ridiculed so long about it, that I am without common patience. So I must beg you to pity me, and pray for liberty of conscience to all.*[23]

5. Using the state church for civil functions

Largely forgotten in our time is the widespread practice in the colonial era of civil government devolving certain civil administrative functions to the state churches. These included social welfare, education, marriage, and the creation and maintenance of important public records, such as birth, burial, and marriage records. The church was also tasked with prosecuting certain moral offenses, and of giving a regular accounting of such to the civil government. This followed a similar pattern, well established in Europe.[24]

6. Limiting political participation to members of the state church

Holding public office in England (during colonial times),

whether that be civil, military, academic, or municipal, without membership in the Church of England was impermissible. Similarly religious restrictions on the right to vote or the qualification for holding a public office were imposed in almost every colony.[25] Even after Independence, every state but Virginia had religious grounds for determining qualification for public office.[26]

What Is the Meaning of This?

For modern readers, these six defining attributes lift the veil and allow us to see the reality of religious establishment in the founding era—a reality commonly understood at that time. In the debates and discussions over the newly drafted Constitution, virtually everyone paying attention knew exactly what it would mean if a national church were to be established. And in the end, they agreed that such an establishment was both unwise and undesirable—from this understanding came the Establishment Clause.

And here is another point:

> **To argue that the Founders intended the Establishment Clause of the First Amendment to mean anything more than prohibiting the establishment of a national church is merely personal preference, not plausible history. To further argue that the Founders did not understand the unique characteristics and implications of religious establishment is absolutely preposterous.**

Yet others *have* argued (with straight faces, no doubt) that establishment, in fact, meant something altogether different. And that is the story of how we have been purposefully diverted from the well-reasoned intent of the Founders onto a highway leading to national delusion.

THE ESTABLISHMENT CLAUSE WRONGLY APPLIED

"Mr. Speaker (or Mr. President), I rise to ask unanimous consent to revise and extend my remarks."

With this Capitol Hill formality, members of the House and Senate routinely "go the well" of their respective chambers to correct mistakes they made in previous remarks. In this manner, what they really said never makes it into the Congressional Record, just a carefully edited version providing another Washington, D.C. staple: plausible deniability. But lest we forget, this shallow (but largely inoffensive) device also provides another enormous benefit to the cause of democratic government among free peoples: they get to talk more. And presumably later revise and extend those additional remarks, advancing the noble cause of retrogressive debate, which will continue until the sun explodes (or more biblically, until Jesus returns).

A Court Unhinged

In these latter days, a far more mendacious and tyrannical variant of "revise and extend" can be found in the decisions of the Supreme Court. But the metaphor breaks down (as metaphors invariably do) in that the Supreme Court is not revising and extending its own jurisprudence; it is revising and extending settled law—and in doing so, often stands precedent on its head.

Notwithstanding the history of the Establishment Clause above, our friends at the National Paralegal College (and others) have decided that the Establishment Clause was intended to *prevent any governmental endorsement or support of religion.*[27] Nice. Very succinct—and completely wrong.

If you remember nothing else from this chapter, please hold onto this.

The goal of the Establishment Clause was to ensure

that no one religion would be favored over another and to protect religious groups from unfair treatment by the federal government.

This was the clear and measured intent of the framers of the Constitution. No other interpretation has historical or even logical support. So how did we get so far off track?

The Wrong Standard—The Wrong Test

For 158 years after the adoption of the Constitution, the federal government seemed to have no great difficulty in understanding and applying the Establishment Clause, with the federal courts largely refraining from even trying to define religion. All that changed in 1947, in the Supreme Court case: *Everson v. Board of Education*.[28] The world does not need another book on the subject, so let's confine ourselves to the essentials.[29]

1. The facts of the case

A New Jersey law allowed reimbursements of money to parents who sent their children to school on buses operated by the public transportation system. Children who attended Catholic schools also qualified for this transportation subsidy.

2. The legal question

Did the New Jersey statute violate the Establishment Clause of the First Amendment as made applicable to the states through the Fourteenth Amendment?

3. The decision

A divided Court held that the law did *not* violate the Constitution. In affirming the judgment of the Court of Appeals, the

Supreme Court found the statute was not unconstitutional because it was designed to provide a benefit to the parents of all school children, distinct from any religious function in which the children engaged.

After detailing the history and importance of the Establishment Clause, Justice Hugo Black (writing for the majority) argued that services like busing and police and fire protection for parochial schools are "separate and so indisputably marked off from the religious function" that for the state to provide them would not violate the First Amendment. The law did not pay money to parochial schools, nor did it support them directly in any way. It was simply a law enacted as a "general program" to assist parents of all religions with getting their children to school.

Win the Battle Lose the War

Even though the Court ruled the New Jersey law did not violate the Establishment Clause, Justice Black's opinion was memorable. He argued from a letter sent by President Thomas Jefferson to the Danbury Baptist Association, which reads in part:

> *Believing with you that religion is a matter which lies solely between Man & his God, that he owes account to none other for his faith or his worship, that the legitimate powers of government reach actions only, & not opinions, I contemplate with sovereign reverence that act of the whole American people which declared that their legislature should "make no law respecting an establishment of religion, or prohibiting the free exercise thereof," thus building a wall of separation between Church & State.*[30]

Justice Black argued:

> *The "establishment of religion" clause of the First*

Amendment means at least this: Neither a state nor the Federal Government can set up a church. Neither can pass laws which aid one religion, aid all religions or prefer one religion over another . . . In the words of Jefferson, the clause against establishment of religion by law was intended to erect "a wall of separation between Church and State." [31]

It was later shown that Justice Black was likely guided (directed?) by the American Civil Liberties Union (ACLU) in developing the "wall" language. In a previously filed *amicus* brief in the *Everson* case, the ACLU wrote:

[The statute] constitutes a definite crack in the wall of separation between church and state. Such cracks have a tendency to widen beyond repair unless promptly sealed up. [32]

So while Justice Black's sweeping argument in *Everson* was not used against the church in this particular case, his use of Jefferson's wall metaphor eventually won the day. The high court's subsequent Establishment Clause interpretations were clearly marked by this turning point. It reflected a broad shift in interpretation that would influence and guide the Court's decisions for decades. Not that other Justices did not continue to push back:

Associate Justice Stanley Reed:

A rule of law should not be drawn from a figure of speech. [33]

Associate Justice Potter Stewart:

[The court] is not responsibly aided by the uncritical invocation of metaphors like the "wall of separation," a phrase nowhere to be found in the Constitution. [34]

Religious Bigotry

Years later, Justice Black's personal bigotry came to light. Black was a liberal Unitarian with a decidedly hostile prejudice against Roman Catholics and other Christians with orthodox beliefs. He also was a one-time member of the Ku Klux Klan, leading one commentator to note: "This doctrine, born of bigotry, should be buried now."[35]

As Jefferson scholar Daniel Dreisbach put it: "What we have is not really Jefferson's wall, but Supreme Court Justice Hugo Black's wall." [36]

The Establishment Clause Reinvented

Other important changes followed *Everson*. Until the 1960s, the courts typically viewed religion in theistic terms. In 1890 the U.S. Supreme Court (*Davis v. Beason*) considered the term religion to be a "reference to one's views of his relations to his Creator, and to the obligations they impose of reverence for his being and character, and of obedience to his will."[37]

In the 1960s, the Court expanded its view of religion. In its 1961 decision *Torcaso v. Watkins*, the Court stated that the Establishment Clause prevents government from aiding "those religions based on a belief in the existence of God as against those religions founded on different beliefs." In a footnote, the Court clarified that this principle extended to "religions in this country, which do not teach what would generally be considered a belief in the existence of God . . . Buddhism, Taoism, Ethical Culture, Secular Humanism and others." [38]

Perhaps the most significant change in the aftermath of *Everson* is that modern constitutional doctrine shifted to using the concept of "advancement of religion" (the so-called Lemon test[39]) as its test for religious establishment, whereas "control" was the central determining factor of establishment in the founding era—and for 158 years under our Constitution.

TWELVE PILLARS OF INTENT

Discovering the intent of the Founders is not that difficult:

May it please your lordships, what did I hear read? Did I hear an expression that these men, whom your worships are about to try for misdemeanor, are charged with preaching the Gospel of the Son of God?[40] (Patrick Henry, 1768)

That religion, or the duty which we owe to our Creator, and the manner of discharging it, can be directed only by reason and conviction, not by force or violence; and therefore all men are equally entitled to the free exercise of religion, according to the dictates of conscience; and that it is the mutual duty of all to practice Christian forbearance, love, and charity towards each other.[41] (James Mason, 1776)

There is not a shadow of right in the general government to intermeddle with religion. Its least interference with it would be a most flagrant usurpation. I can appeal to my uniform conduct on this subject, that I have warmly supported religious freedom.[42] (James Madison, 1788)

If I could have entertained the slightest apprehension that the Constitution framed in the Convention, where I had the honor to preside, might possibly endanger the religious rights of any ecclesiastical society, certainly I would never have placed my signature to it.[43] (George Washington, May 10, 1789)

We have no government armed with power capable of contending with human passions unbridled by morality and religion. Avarice, ambition, revenge, or gallantry would break the strongest cords of our Constitution as a whale goes through a net. Our Constitution was made only for a moral and religious people. It is wholly inadequate to the government of any other.[44] (John Adams, 1798)

In matters of religion I have considered that its free exercise is placed by the Constitution independent of the powers of the General Government. I have therefore undertaken, on no occasion, to prescribe the religious exercise suited to it; but have left them, as the Constitution found them, under the direction of state and church authorities by the several religious societies.[45] (Thomas Jefferson, 1805)

Providence has given to our people the choice of their rulers, and it is the duty, as well as the privilege and interest of our Christian Nation, to select and prefer Christians for their rulers.[46] (First Chief Justice of the Supreme Court John Jay, 1816)

The highest, the transcendent glory of the American Revolution was this—it connected, in one indissoluble bond, the principles of civil government with the precepts of Christianity.[47] (John Quincy Adams, 1837)

Let us not forget the religious character of our origin. Our fathers were brought hither by their high veneration for the Christian religion. They journeyed by its light, and labored in its hope. They sought to incorporate its principles with the elements of their society, and to diffuse its influence through all their institutions, civil, political, or literary.[48] (Daniel Webster, 1851)

The First Amendment, however, does not say that in every respect there shall be a separation of Church and State. Rather, it studiously defines the manner, the specific ways, in which there shall be no concert or union or dependency one on the other. That is the common sense of the matter. Otherwise the state and religion would be aliens to each other—hostile, suspicious, and even unfriendly.[49] (Supreme Court Justice William O. Douglas, 1952)

In light of the unambiguous and unbroken history of more than 200 years, there can be no doubt that the practice of opening legislative sessions with prayer has become part of the fabric of our society. To invoke Divine guidance on a public body entrusted with making the laws is not, in these circumstances, an establishment of religion or a step toward establishment. It is simply a tolerable acknowledgement of beliefs widely held among the people of this country.[50] (Supreme Court Chief Justice Warren Burger, 1983)

It is impossible to build sound constitutional doctrine upon a mistaken understanding of Constitutional history . . . The establishment clause has been expressly freighted with Jefferson's misleading metaphor for nearly forty years . . . There is simply no historical foundation for the proposition that the framers intended to build a wall of separation [between church and state] . . . The recent court decisions are in no way based on either the language or the intent of the framers.[51] (Supreme Court Justice William Rehnquist, 1985)

MAYBE THE FOUNDERS WERE WRONG

For the sake of fairness, let's turn our attention to one more argument against an originalist interpretation of the First Amendment. As you will see, it's an archetypal liberal argument with maximum speculation, minimum substance, and the exact wrong conclusion. But here goes.

The evidence for the original intent of the Founders with respect to religious freedom is so clear and so well documented that socialist establishmentarians now signal a new strategy in opposing an originalist interpretation of the First Amendment. Since they cannot argue against what the Founders actually said (or even intended) some liberal commentators now make an argument that is clean and simple: the Founders were wrong.[52][53]

This is refreshing honesty on the part of liberals and progressive socialists, because in saying the Founders were wrong they must stipulate to what the Founders actually said and intended. This is important because the Founders intended to protect the free exercise of religion, and *this* is the very thing these critics say was "wrong."

This liberal stipulation also is long-overdue recognition that these were thoughtful (in some cases brilliant) men who had carefully studied the histories of every notable government as preparation for framing a new one. Furthermore, these were notable men recognized for their character and reputation, as well as their intellect. As serious thinkers they each had their private ideas on the Constitution, but those private ideas were publically debated. The 85 published *Federalist Papers* alone are testament to the vigorous and public nature of that debate. Our form of government was not handed down from Mount Olympus, nor was it arranged in some smoke-filled room shaped by a handful of dealmakers.

The Founders lived in momentous times. Many had a price on their heads during the Revolution. Having weathered that great storm by the grace of God in which they pledged to one another "their lives, their fortunes, and their sacred honor," they did not embrace new ideas without research, debate, and prayers for wisdom from on high.

If It's Wrong—Fix It

Yet, if the Founders *were* in fact wrong, as some modern critics allege, the Constitution itself provides the corrective: the amendment process found in Article V. As to the amendment procedure itself, it is not overly complicated, but (by design) it is demanding. Only proposed amendments that are well reasoned and have the broadest public support can be considered and ratified. James Madison, writing in *Federalist Paper #43*, argued that the amendment process embodied two important protections:

> *It guards equally against that extreme facility which would render the Constitution too mutable; and that extreme difficulty which might perpetuate its discovered faults.*[54]

So the Founders recognized the need for a prudent amendment process—one that ensured a measure of flexibility to remedy error, but at the same time allowed duly enacted laws to remain unchanged for a time so that their full force and effect might be felt.

As an aside, I personally believe the Founders were wrong on the question of lifetime appointments for federal judges and justices.[55] Here is a clear example of the Law of Unintended Consequences at work. The framers of the Constitution hoped that lifetime appointments would insulate judges from the populism and political forces that would animate many elected representatives. Instead we have an almost completely unaccountable judiciary that has slipped the bonds of its constitutional mandate and taken unto itself (in some cases) the law-making function intended only for the people, through their elected representatives. The same-sex marriage decision is a perfect example of this judicial usurpation and tyranny.

Therefore, for opponents who think free exercise of religion was a mistake, the amendment process is open to them. Not that they are likely to bother when they can always turn to a tyrannical court to effect the change they want.

IMPORTANT KEYS TO SEPARATION

The Intended Wall

Jefferson's metaphor of a wall of separation was not completely wrong. This is well expressed in the opening stanza of a timeless hymn:

> *The Church's one foundation*
> *Is Jesus Christ her Lord,*
> *She is His new creation*
> *By water and the Word.*
> *From heaven He came and sought her*
> *To be His holy bride;*
> *With His own blood He bought her*
> *And for her life He died*

The church is a blood-bought community of believers, called out of the world to be the people of God. Yet, individual believers are members of both the City of God (the heavenly city) and the City of Man (the earthly city), as outlined by St. Augustine. Individual believers must submit to civil government because it also is ordained by God. But individual believers owe no submission to government in matters of faith. As Peter and John said to the Sanhedrin: "Whether it is right in the sight of God to listen to you more than to God, you judge. For we cannot help but declare what we have seen and heard" (Acts 4:19-20).

Accordingly, there is (and should always be) a great wall separating human government from the affairs and work of the church. It is a wall founded upon the sovereignty of God. Governments have no legitimate role meddling in the church's work, worship, or practices—and especially not in its doctrine and its polity. To what extent the Founders ever thought in terms of Jefferson's wall metaphor, we do not know. We do know that Jefferson was 3,700 miles away in France when the Constitution was drafted.

The Unintended Wall

It is inarguable that the speeches, books, and letters of the Founders (even the supposed deists) in no way contemplate or anticipate the creation of a secular state. The tortured modern notion that Jefferson's wall metaphor expressed some consensus that the values, precepts, and ideals of the Christian religion should be kept from having any influence on our federal government is manifestly absurd. That frail hypothesis has long since been crushed under the weight of historical documentation. Even a brief walk among the historic government buildings of Washington, D.C. (where those buildings are prominently marked with biblical texts, allusions, references, and citations) refutes this ludicrous notion, as quickly as the sunlight dissipates the shadows.

The Silent Public Square

We have our current First Amendment jurisprudence because an unaccountable court says it should be so. The aim is not merely the separation of church and state, but the separation of the church from the public square. Government and the forces of secularism see establishment everywhere, even when the argument is manifestly nonsensical in light of what religious establishment actually was. Yet while government and cultural bullies are ever vigilant to spot even imaginary establishment, the same governments seems totally insensate to transgressions of the Free Exercise clause. Where is

Jefferson's wall when you need it?

The true end and aim of separation is to silence the Gospel of Jesus Christ. No evenhanded person would ever conclude that students praying before a football game, or a ten-year-old reading her Bible on the lunch break at school were part of an effort to establish a state church. The whole notion violates the so-called "reasonable man" standard in common law. Would a reasonable man (or woman) think that a schoolboy wearing his "Christ is the Answer" tee-shirt or a schoolgirl wearing her "I Play for an Audience of One" tee-shirt are an establishment of a government church? Not a chance.

Yet the "higher calling" of modern secular (especially socialist) governments is the suppression of dissent. The end and aim of separation is to silence the Gospel of Jesus Christ—and to enforce a Silent Public Square.

WHAT WE MUST REMEMBER ABOUT SEPARATION

Our Rights Come from God

No judge or justice of any court has a constitutional mandate to decide the nature or extent of religious practice in the public square.

God Established Spheres of Authority

While we think of the separation of powers enshrined in our Constitution as a (relatively) modern concept, it is in some sense a creation ordinance, in that God divinely ordained the spheres of legitimate authority for His creation. Civil government, also ordained by God, has no authority over Christ and His church—beyond what God allows in His word.

The Bill of Rights Restricts the Power of Government

The central failure of First Amendment jurisprudence in the last 90 years has been a seemingly premeditated amnesia regarding the truth that the Bill of Rights embodies restrictions on the power of Congress (and now the states via the 14th Amendment).

The intent and purposes of the Bill of Rights are self-evident from the wording. In understanding how to apply the First Amendment, you only need understand three things:

> *Congress shall make no law.*
> *Congress shall make no law.*
> *Congress shall make no law.*

Please forgive the redundancies in making this point. But it cannot be said too often that each of the ten amendments comprising the Bill of Rights is a restriction on the power of the federal government and the states. Yes, we are citizens of a heavenly city and at the same time citizens of an earthly city. And, yes, we must obey the legitimate dictates of civil government. But there is a place where civil government slips the bonds of its legitimate authority. At that place, the choice for every Christian becomes clear.

The False Modern Doctrine of Establishment

The Establishment Clause in the First Amendment of the Constitution was included and adopted to address a specific issue in the founding era—the presence of state-established churches in a majority of the original 13 colonies. The only goal of the Establishment Clause was to ensure that no one religion would be favored over another and to protect religious groups from unfair treatment by the federal government.

WHAT WE MUST DO ABOUT SEPARATION

The impact of an oppressive jurisprudence on religious freedom would make a book in itself. We cannot speak adequately to it here. But we can consider our response to circumstance beyond our control. When you think of it, a good deal of life is beyond our control, yet we make choices every day, doing what we can.

So what about religious free speech? In the end, the question of religious establishment is something of a canard—it is not an insubstantial issue, it's just not the real issue. The real issue is: Will you speak or remain silent? Will you engage the marketplace of ideas with the mind of Christ or withdraw? Will you live out your faith or retreat to your stained glass ghetto? What will you do? Here are a few things to consider.

1. Consider your citizenship in the City of God[56]

What does it mean in the here and now? The scripture says we look forward to a city with foundations whose architect and builder is God. Our heavenly home may be a ways off, but we are to live today in light of that future dwelling in the presence of God. As Francis Schaeffer said: "How then should we live?" Well, simply put: we should live for Christ—in the public square as much as in the comfort of our homes and churches. Besides, if we will not engage the public square with the mind of Christ, how long will our churches and homes remain secure?

2. Consider your citizenship in the City of Man

What about civil disobedience? We have an obligation to obey the legitimate laws of civil government, for God also established it. Yet when Peter and John stood before the Sanhedrin, who commanded that they no longer "teach in this name" they replied:

"Whether it is right in the sight of God to listen to you rather than to God, you must judge." Few of us have yet reached that place of choosing, but it seems highly likely that we will. We should remember that one reported slogan of the American Revolution was: No king but King Jesus.

3. Consider the freedoms we still have

As citizens of both cities, we have obligations and opportunities in both. We still live in a constitutional republic with more religious freedom than any other nation in the world. We still have elected representatives. Elections do matter. There are no perfect candidates, but your electoral participation can change the direction of a government in rebellion against God. The president can appoint Supreme Court justices committed to an originalist understanding of the Constitution.

As citizens of the City of God, we must *be* and *do*. We must be the people of God, and we must do the work of the kingdom. As citizens of the City of Man also, we must *be* and *do*. We must be the salt of the earth and the light of the world, and we must do the good work of loving neighbor and friend. A friend cares for his neighbors' freedom as part of an overall concern for their welfare.

The "wall of separation between Church and State" is a Metaphor based on bad history, metaphor which has proved useless as a guide to judging. It should be frankly and explicitly abandoned.[57]

(Supreme Court Justice William Rehnquist)

CHAPTER TWO

EXECUTIVE OVERREACH
The Insanity of Concentrated Executive Power

They said to him: "You are old and your sons
do not walk in your ways. Now, install for us
a king to govern us like all the nations."

(1 Samuel 8:5)

When the legislative and executive powers are
united in the same person, or in the same body of
magistrates, there can be no liberty.[58]

(Charles de Secondat, Baron de Montesquieu)

On his robe and on his thigh he has a name
written: King of kings and Lord of lords.

(Revelation 19:16)

The imperial presidency, executive overreach, executive abuse, or just plain old progressive socialism—whatever you choose to call it—in our day it is unprecedented in its scope and scale. Like some breathtaking *blitzkrieg* of executive usurpation, the last seven years (arguably the last fifteen years) have been the boldest assault on the Constitution's separation of powers since Franklin Delano Roosevelt.

In less than one biblical generation, our Constitution stands in tatters, and some say our nation stands at a tipping point—either tyranny or a return to constitutional government. How did we get here? How could this happen in the land of the free and the home of the brave?

BIBLICAL ROOTS OF THE SEPARATION OF POWERS

The political and legal doctrine of what we now call the "separation of powers" has deep historical roots. While some would attribute its heritage to John Locke or Charles Montesquieu, others look further back to the philosophers of ancient Greece. Still others say we must look even further back to ancient Israel to see its first clear appearing.[59]

Indeed it is with Moses that we see the birth pains of the separation of powers. After the exodus from Egypt, Moses' father-in-law Jethro comes to meet with him in the wilderness. When Jethro observes Moses wearing himself out judging the disputes of the people, he charges Moses to consider whether God would have it done differently. He says:

> *Now listen to me, I will advise you, and may God be with you: You be a representative for the people to God so that you may bring their disputes to God. And you shall teach them the statutes and laws and shall show them the way in which they must walk and the work that they must do. Moreover, you shall*

choose out of all the people capable men who fear
God, men of truth, hating dishonest gain, and place
these men over them, to be rulers of thousands,
rulers of hundreds, rulers of fifties, and rulers of
tens. Let them judge the people at all times, and let it
be that every difficult matter they shall bring to you,
but every small matter they shall judge, so that it
will be easier for you, and they will bear the burden
with you (Exodus 18:19-22) [emphasis added].

So Moses chooses a cohort of judges—capable men chosen
from out of the people—to share the burden of judging the disputes
of the people. The judicial function thereby is separated out of the
leadership function, and the officers of the judicial function are
chosen from *out of the people.* In this governing structure God
retains for Himself the role of Lawgiver and King, with Moses
serving as a minister of God to the people.

Later in Israel's history—at the end of the time of the Judges—
the people come to Samuel demanding a king. Samuel (at God's
direction) issues a prophetic warning to the people detailing for
them the abuses they would face under a king:

And he said, "This will be the judgment concerning
the king who will reign over you: Your sons he
will take in order to place them for himself in his
chariots and as his horsemen, and they will run
before his chariot, and in order to assign for himself
captains of thousands and captains of fifties, and to
plow his ground, and to gather in his harvest, and
to make his weapons of war and the equipment
of his chariots. And your daughters he will take
for perfumers, and cooks, and bakers. And your
choicest fields, and vineyards, and olive groves he
will take and give them to his servants. And of your
seed fields and your vineyards he will take a tenth
of their harvest and will give it to his high officials

and to his servants. And your menservants and your maidservants, and the best of your young men and asses he will take and make do his work. Your flocks he will take a tenth of, but you will be his for slaves. And you will cry out in that day because of your king, whom you have chosen for yourselves, but the Lord will not answer you in that day"
(1 Samuel 8:11-18).

Yet the people would not be denied, so God gave Israel a king (Saul), and a clearer separation of powers emerges: king and judge, with God continuing as the sole Lawgiver in Israel.

Worth noting is that this pattern of government is a reflection of God's revelation of Himself in Scripture: Lawgiver, Judge, and King (see Isaiah 33:22). Only in Christ are all three earthly roles combined. And Jesus willingly took on a fourth role: the sacrificial offering. He became the very sacrifice that satisfied the just requirements of the law, making atonement for those who would trust in Him.

WHY A SEPARATION OF POWERS?

This governing structure first observed in ancient Israel is the functional pattern given to us by the Founders, with the powers within our constitutional framework separated between legislative (Congress), judicial (the federal courts), and executive (the president). These powers are separated because the Founders wisely recognized two significant forces that historically have led back to tyranny: 1) the sinful nature of man, and 2) the corrupting influences of concentrated power.

WHY CHECKS AND BALANCES?

The framers of the Constitution were persuaded that these

corrupting forces (sin and concentrated power) would be so difficult to mitigate that additional constraints were needed. These additional constraints they added by providing potent checks and balances, whereby one branch of government can (in certain cases) limit or overturn the actions of another. The framers placed a further limitation on corrupting influences by providing a constitutional process for removal from office which we call impeachment.

WHY GO TO SUCH GREAT LENGTHS?

In adding such powerful constraints to limit the effects of concentrated power, the framers of the Constitution were heeding the maxim of Lord John Dahlberg-Acton who said:

> *Power tends to corrupt and absolute power corrupts absolutely. Great men are almost always bad men, even when they exercise influence and not authority; still more when you superadd the tendency of the certainty of corruption by authority.*[60]

THE FIRST GREAT USURPATION

In looking at how concentrated power leads to usurpation, James Madison noted:

> *I believe there are more instances of the abridgment of the freedom of the people by gradual and silent encroachments of those in power than by violent and sudden usurpations.*[61]

And interestingly, it was Madison who faced down the first great effort at the usurpation of political power under our Constitution. This first test came in the 1803 case of *Marbury v. Madison*. In it the Supreme Court claimed the right to invalidate legislation based upon whether or not it accorded with the Constitution—what we now call judicial review.

It is worth noting that the power of judicial review is nowhere mentioned in the Constitution. Thomas Jefferson warned that such a power would lead to a form of despotism:

> *The Constitution . . . meant that its coordinate branches should be checks on each other. But the opinion which gives to the judges the right to decide what laws are constitutional and what not, not only for themselves in their own sphere of action but for the Legislature and Executive also in their spheres, would make the Judiciary a despotic branch.*[62]

Based upon Justice Marshall's arguments, the Supreme Court held that the Constitution was "the fundamental and paramount law of the nation" and that "an act of the legislature repugnant to the constitution is void."[63]

In the end, President James Madison ignored the Supreme Court's decision in *Marbury*. However, in a classic "win the battle lose the war scenario" the power of the federal judiciary has expanded dramatically over time (with judicial review intact), showing the expressed concerns of Thomas Jefferson and others to be prescient.

USURPATION IN THE EXECUTIVE BRANCH

A Definition

"A usurper is an illegitimate or controversial claimant to power, often but not always in a monarchy. This may include a person who succeeds in establishing himself as a monarch without inheriting the throne or any other person exercising authority unconstitutionally. A person who takes the power of the country for himself or herself at the expense of the people. It may also be applied to an official acting *ultra vires*, outside his authority or jurisdiction."[64]

Some say this definition well-describes the *modus operandi* of the present executive branch administration. But why is it generally the executive branch that overreaches?

Why the Executive Branch?

Abuse of authority in the executive branch is more common under our Constitution for the simple reason that executive branch entities are better positioned to seize opportunities to expand their power base by virtue of their ability to respond quickly to fast moving, rapidly changing situations.[65]

As Rahm Emmanuel, then Chief of Staff for President-elect Obama put it:

> *You never let a serious crisis go to waste. And what I mean by that—it's an opportunity to do things you think you could not do before.*[66]

The point being that during times of emergency necessitating quick responses, the executive branch can act unilaterally. By contrast (and by design) the legislative branch moves at a deliberate, measured pace. Quick law seldom is good law. And the judiciary has no independent power to initiate action at all. By definition it rules upon actions filed in the courts—generally at a seemingly glacial pace.

SLIPPING THE BONDS OF EXECUTIVE LIMITATIONS

A Test of Character

As in all other things, the tendency of any particular presidential administration to exceed its constitutional limitations is determined by the tone set by the president. Speaking of this presidential tendency toward usurpation, Abraham Lincoln said:

> *Nearly all men can stand adversity, but if you want to test a man's character, give him power.*[67]

And this is the heart and soul of executive overreach and abuse of authority: the question of character. All presidents have self-referential and sinful tendencies. But on this point Lord Acton (quoted above) often is misquoted. The common misquote is that "power corrupts; absolute power corrupts absolutely." But Lord Acton did not say that. He said: "power *tends* to corrupt" [emphasis added]. Power has a tendency to corrupt; character is the bulwark standing between temptation and usurpation.

Oath Breakers

The Scriptures speak of sins as doing things that should not be done, as well as omitting things that should not be neglected. In other words, we can sin actively or passively. In the same manner executive abuse of authority and responsibility can be both active and passive.

On Inauguration Day the President of the United States stands on the west front of the Capitol Building to take his oath of office. The Chief Justice of the Supreme Court administers that oath as follows:

> *I do solemnly swear (or affirm) that I will faithfully execute the Office of President of the United States, and will to the best of my ability, preserve, protect and defend the Constitution of the United States.*[68]

The imperial presidency is marked by an oath-breaking usurpation that is both passive and active. Both instances are an abuse of executive authority. A president who clutches for powers not accorded in the Constitution is abusive by usurpation. A president refusing to act when duly enacted laws or regulations require it is abusive by neglect—which is only another species of usurpation.

This question of oath breaking is no small matter. The Scriptures speak to it clearly and forcefully:

> *If a man vows a vow to the Lord, or swears an* **oath** *to bind himself with a bond, he will not break his word. He will do according to all that proceeds out of his mouth* (Numbers 30:2).

> *Let none of you consider evil plans in your heart against your neighbor, and do not love false* **oaths,** *for I hate all these things, says the Lord* (Zechariah 8:17).

Active Oath Breaking

In our system of government, a president arrogating to himself legislative or judicial authority *actively* breaks his oath of office, in which he pledged to uphold the Constitution.

Active usurpation generally takes two forms: 1) using executive orders to get around the authority of Congress, and 2) using the regulatory process to make new law, completely by-passing Congress and the people, refusing even a reasonable measure of accountability.

Passive Oath Breaking

Even more contemptible than a president who is an active oath breaker is the president whose oath breaking is passive. An active usurper can see his administration defunded by Congress and its illegitimate actions challenged in the courts.

But when a president refuses to enforce duly enacted laws

and regulations simply because he chooses not to, he is a usurper of the worst order. For in these instances he has usurped and unilaterally overturned the will of the people (through their elected representatives) by his willful and deliberate inaction.

Michael McConnell, a former federal judge who is now a professor of law and director of the Constitutional Law Center at Stanford Law School, describes this abuse as unilateral suspension of law:

> *While the president does have substantial discretion about how to enforce a law, he has no discretion about* <u>*whether*</u> *to do so . . . Of all the stretches of executive power Americans have seen in the past few years, the president's unilateral suspension of statutes may have the most disturbing long-term effects* [emphasis in original].[69]

A president willfully ignoring duly enacted laws, regulations, or court decisions is little more than a tyrant who disregards and disrespects the authority of "we the people." For this reason alone the passive oath breaker is the more disreputable offender.

THE 44ᵀᴴ PRESIDENT

With the current administration this question of executive overreach can be viewed either as a subject of profound irony or one of masterful mendacity. Some would say: both.

In 2008, then-candidate Obama campaigned vigorously against what he claimed was the imperial presidency of George W. Bush. At a gathering of supporters, Obama claimed that one of America's "<u>biggest problems</u>" involved "George Bush trying to bring more and more power into the executive branch and not go through Congress at all."[70] President Obama went further when repeatedly he told campaign audiences that sweeping unilateral moves would be a violation of constitutional standards.

While the Constitution grants the Congress the authority to make law and the president the authority to enforce the law, it does not give the president the power to suspend a law or grant waivers for its requirements. Yet President Obama has done this repeatedly on matters as disparate as: immigration, heath care, welfare, education, drug policy.[71] According to columnist George Will, President Obama has suspended, waived, and rewritten many laws, including the Affordable Care Act.[72]

Ah well, apparently that was then, and this is now. In observing not just the number but the character and scope of President Obama's executive orders, former House Majority Leader Eric Cantor said:

> *The president's dangerous search for expanded powers appears to be endless.*[73]

While the Obama administration has passively refused to defend duly enacted laws in court before, it's most spectacular passive usurpation is its willful and deliberate refusal to enforce immigration law. Federal law requires anyone in the country illegally to be deported, but seeing itself as above the law (some would say as a law unto itself) the Obama administration refuses to enforce the existing law.[74] Can someone say "oath-breaker?"

What Americans Want?

Never before in American history has one presidential administration so willfully and forcefully disregarded the Constitution. And here are two quotes emblematic of President Obama's personal justification for doing so:

> *We're not just going to be waiting around for legislation in order to make sure that we're providing Americans the kind of help they need. I've got a pen,*

and I've got a phone.[75]

The American people don't want me just standing around twiddling my thumbs and waiting for Congress to get something done.[76]

These words are classic Obama self-referential justification. They seem layered with the familiar narcissism, but these are in essence the words of an oath-breaker, of someone who sees the Constitution as an elective guide to action. These also are the words of one who can apparently walk past the graves at Arlington Cemetery without a thought for those who gave their lives in defense of the Constitution and of freedom. In the end these are the words of tyranny.

IMPORTANT KEYS TO EXECUTIVE OVERREACH

1. The imperial presidency is perfectly in keeping with socialism

Socialism seeks to consolidate all power in the hands of the state—whether that be in the hands of few (as in an oligarchy) or in the hands of one (as in a dictator). As the separation of powers breaks down, and the established checks and balances atrophy from disuse, power continues to concentrate in the branch of government able to move quickest. Deepening dependency on government awaits only the "suitable" crisis to emerge, leading us to see government *of, by,* and *for* the people vanish into the mists of history. Sound too dramatic for you? Then spend an hour or two looking at the history of Germany before World War II. Arguably, it all began with a breakdown in the separation of powers.

As President Dwight Eisenhower observed:

Every step we take towards making the State our

Caretaker of our lives, by that much we move toward making the State our Master.[77]

2. Usurpation ultimately destroys fundamental freedoms

With the weakening of the separation of powers comes a generalized weakening of resistance to even patently obvious encroachment and usurpation. As the branch of government best able to move quickly and unilaterally, the executive branch will increasingly face only verbal opposition, with legislative and judicial remedies stretching off into a future that may never arrive. Gone (possibly more quickly than you can imagine) will be the five freedoms of the First Amendment: religion, speech, press, assembly, and petition.

As President John Adams noted:

> *The jaws of power are always open to devour, and her arm is always stretched out, if possible, to destroy the freedom of thinking, speaking, and writing.*[78]

WHAT WE MUST REMEMBER ABOUT EXECUTIVE OVERREACH

1. In our system of government, we have no king

The Scriptures require that we obey the civil authorities that God places over us. In the ancient world, that meant the king and his representatives. What then, in a constitutional republic, is our biblical duty to obey those God has placed in authority over us? It is obedience to the Constitution. Not to the president.

As President Theodore Roosevelt describes it:

> *Patriotism means to stand by the country. It does not mean to stand by the President or any other public*

official save exactly to the degree in which he himself stands by the country. It is patriotic to support him insofar as he efficiently serves the country. It is unpatriotic not to oppose him to the exact extent that by inefficiency or otherwise he fails in his duty to stand by the country.[79]

2. "We the people" must defend the constitution

The Constitution, together with the Declaration of Independence, establishes "we the people" as the ultimate defender of the Constitution.

As President Abraham Lincoln stated:

> *We the People are the rightful masters of both Congress and the Courts—not to overthrow the Constitution, but to overthrow the men who pervert the Constitution.*[80]

WHAT WE MUST DO ABOUT EXECUTIVE OVERREACH

Elections Matter

With the constitutional balance of powers so dramatically tilted toward executive power, choosing the next president might mean the difference between constitutional government and tyranny.

As President Andrew Jackson affirmed:

> *The great constitutional corrective in the hands of the people against usurpation of power, or corruption by their agents is the right of suffrage; and this when used with calmness and deliberation will prove strong enough.*[81]

Checks and Balances

The current constitutional imbalance (executive overreach) must be counteracted by a concerted effort by the federal judiciary and the Congress to rein in executive power that improperly usurps Congress's authority to make law.

As President James Madison observed:

> *In framing a government, which is to be administered by men over men, the great difficulty is this: You must first enable the government to control the governed; and in the next place, oblige it to control itself.*[82]

The irony here should be obvious. We must look to a judicial branch that has itself repeatedly usurped the legislative authority of Congress and the people. A usurping judicial branch must rein in a usurping executive branch.

The accumulation of all powers, legislative, executive, and judiciary, into the same hands, whether of one, a few, or many, and whether hereditary, self-appointed, or elective, may be justly pronounced the very definition of tyranny.[83]

(James Madison)

CHAPTER THREE

THE DECEIT OF KARL MARX
The Insanity of Our Reckless Embrace of Socialism

It's hard to believe that the United States, having resisted the siren song of socialism during its entire 20th century heyday, should suddenly succumb to its charms a generation after its intellectual demise.[84]

(Political commentator, Charles Krauthammer)

The state is that great fiction by which everyone tries to live at the expense of everyone else.[85]

(Political economist, Frederic Bastiat)

There is not a square inch in the whole domain of our human existence over which Christ, who is Sovereign over all, does not cry, "Mine!" [86]

(Dutch statesman and theologian, Abraham Kuyper)

Less than three decades after the fall of the Berlin Wall, socialism seems to be undergoing something of a revival. So says columnist Michael Tanner of *National Review*.[87] Yet the roots of our most caustic social pathologies can be found in this same lifeless soil: the barren and bitter ground of socialism. By socialism I do not mean vague notions of seeking the general welfare of the people. I mean the reality of socialism; what former Speaker of the House Newt Gingrich called: "a government-dominated, bureaucratically-controlled, politician-dictated way of life."[88]

Many people naively (and to their peril) view socialism as merely an organizing framework for human government—one of many from which we might choose. But that is like saying the guillotine is merely an aid to weight-loss—one of many from which we might choose.

Choose the guillotine for weight-loss and you will surely lose weight. You will also surely die. So also do nations that choose socialism—but not death from the quick flash of a falling blade. They die the slow and agonizing death of moral and cultural decay and disintegration.

But you might ask: Why is this necessarily so? Why do nations that choose socialism ultimately die? Perhaps equally important, we might ask: What is socialism that people would choose it at all?

CHANGING DEFINITIONS

Why Words Matter

The dictionary you choose matters—it really does. This is so because culture will always try to justify itself by redefining and ameliorating the hard edges of the very bad things it does. Sin, for example, is no longer an attitude of a heart in rebellion against God and His revealed word. Instead contemporary culture redefines sin as: poor choices, inappropriate conduct, errors in judgment, personal indiscretions, and the like. The late Senator Daniel Patrick

Moynihan called it "defining deviancy down."[89] I tend to think of it as the euphemistic evasion of veracity. In any event, truth is the usual casualty of these euphemistic evasions, and socialism has not been immune from cultural attempts to substitute a more soothing redefinition.

We can see this by taking a good dictionary off the shelf, or bookmarking its URL. An excellent place to start is the Oxford English Dictionary (OED), which modestly calls itself "the definitive record of the English language."

The first definition of "socialism" in the OED is the most ancient (as we might expect from a historical dictionary), defining it as:

> *The theory of social organization under the social contract.*[90]

Immediately after this somewhat murky definition (with its shadowy reference to the so-called Age of Enlightenment), the OED gives us a time-period quotation about socialism. In this case it's from *The Weekly Wanderer* (Randolph, Vermont), dated June of 1801:

> *How often has this little word (socialism) in genteel arguments occurred, as though the soul of socialism must be transmitted through a prism . . . High in the front [of the prism] see "atheism," and next in rank stands "Tom Paineism."*

Here we see a reference to a long-acknowledged truth (much obscured in our day) that at the heart and soul of socialism is a tenacious and antagonistic atheism. Socialism brings destruction and death to society for the simple reason that it stands fully and unreservedly opposed to the Lord of Life. Subscribing to the notion that human beings are the measure of all things, socialism seeks to elevate the authority of men and women, while at the same time denying any notion of accountability to God.

The second definition of socialism in the OED is more expansive:

*A theory or system of social organization **based on state or collective ownership** and regulation of the means of production, distribution, and exchange for the common benefit of all members of society; advocacy or practice of such a system, esp. as a political movement. Now also: any of various systems of liberal social democracy which retain a commitment to social justice and social reform, or feature some degree of state intervention in the running of the economy* [emphasis added].

Our friends at the Oxford English Dictionary then further illuminate us with a footnote to this larger definition:

*The range of application of the term [socialism] is broad. It is typically understood to involve the elevation of the social position and interests of the working class, **especially through redistribution of land or wealth**, nationalization of industry and services, and the creation of workers' cooperatives. It is sometimes used synonymously with (esp. Soviet) Communism, although in some Marxist contexts it [socialism] is used specifically to denote **a transitional stage between the overthrow of capitalism and the realization of Communism** [emphasis added].*

The Bottom Line

Here then we see the definitive fullness of socialism. It is atheistic, having as its organizing principle the state ownership or control of all productive assets. Its purported ethic is the elevation of the worker, which is accomplished by a Robin Hood-like redistribution of wealth. It is as Frederic Bastiat[91] described it: "legalized plunder." Finally, lest we be deceived, it is viewed as a transitional stage between the overthrow of capitalism and the full realization of Marxist socialism (Communism). Even today, some argue that the abject failure of Soviet-style socialism should not be counted against Marxist socialism.[92] All of this stands in stark contrast to the far more pacific redefinition of socialism in our day.

The Cultural Bait and Switch

To try and capture the cultural shift in redefining socialism, we go to our friends at *Wikipedia: The Free Encyclopedia.* If you don't know how *Wikipedia* works, a word of caution is in order.[93] *Wikipedia* articles are written by a largely anonymous group of volunteers. With a few exceptions, anyone with Internet access can write and make changes to *Wikipedia* articles.

While *Wikipedia* volunteers agree to govern themselves by five fundamental principles that help to ensure the integrity of the articles, one need not wake up Einstein to see there is potential for abuse. So most people take *Wikipedia* as a starting point in researching a topic, not an ending point. But for our purposes (assessing the changing cultural definition of socialism), *Wikipedia* may be a helpful proxy for a broad-based cultural consensus on the theme of socialism.

Here is how *Wikipedia* defines socialism:[94]

> *Socialism is a range of economic and social systems characterised*[95] *by social ownership and democratic control of the means of production; as well as the political ideologies, theories,. and movements that aim at their establishment.*

Nothing Up My Sleeve

I hope you will notice immediately (by sleight of hand) the clever introduction (and substitution) of two *new* definitional terms:

1) social ownership, and 2) democratic control. We will look first at "social ownership," returning to "democratic control" later.

Social ownership. This new expression in *Wikipedia* replaces the historic definitional understanding of "state or collective ownership" of the means of production (as in the OED). From this we might assume that socialism no longer is about state ownership of the productive assets of an economy. However, that would be a dangerous and false assumption, as in reality nothing has changed.

We can see this by taking a closer look at how *Wikipedia* more fully defines "social ownership:"

> *Social ownership refers to the various forms of ownership for the means of production in socialist economic systems; encompassing public ownership, employee ownership, cooperative ownership, citizen ownership of equity and common ownership . . .* **Social ownership of the means of production is the common defining characteristic of all the various forms of socialism** [emphasis added].

Note first that social ownership is said to be the "common defining characteristic of all the various forms of socialism." Second, we should recognize that "social ownership" (at least in the context of contemporary socialism) is largely indistinguishable from "state ownership" in historic socialism—except that it allows for some citizen ownership of "equity." Note well that this (seemingly free market) concept of equity does not provide for any actual citizen ownership of "the means of production," only for some undefined equity interest in them.

As an aside, we would be wise to remain highly skeptical of depending upon socialist definitions of capital market terminology. In this case, an "equity investment" might resemble a visit to *Hotel California*, where it is said that you can check out but you can never leave. This form of "equity" would likely be just another way for socialist governments to convert private property into state assets.

Let's turn our attention now from ownership to control.

Democratic control. The second new (and largely false) term introduced into the *Wikipedia* definition of socialism is "democratic control" of the means of production. Just as we should be wary of socialist definitions of capital market terminology, we also must be exceedingly suspicious of socialist notions of democracy—especially those largely detached from historical reality.

This concept of "democratic control" in a socialistic framework falls into the category of what is called the Big Lie. We attribute the derivation of the Big Lie to Joseph Goebbels, Propaganda Minister to Adolph Hitler, who reportedly said:

> *If you tell a lie big enough and keep repeating it, people will eventually come to believe it.*[96]

The idea of democratic elections in most truly socialist nations comes right out of the Lewis Carroll School of Historical Fantasy. With the exception of a "socialist candidate" here and there (and a few semi-socialist, northern European countries) democratic elections in truly socialist settings are on par with an elaborately staged Kabuki Theater.

A DISTINCTION WITHOUT A DIFFERENCE

We can see from all of this that the "new" socialism is undifferentiated from the old, except that its mendacious marketing department has become far more skilled at shadowing its real intention, which is the state ownership and control of all productive assets. By the way, if you haven't guessed, those productive assets include your money.

The definitive aim of socialism will always be to place mankind (and ultimately the state) in the place of God. And in seeking to dethrone God, socialism seeks nothing more than the accumulation of power. And having accreted all power unto itself, socialism then drops all pretense of preserving freedom, instead demanding subjection to the state in all things.

Why has our national culture seemingly lost its mind? Because in accruing its power, socialism must necessarily destroy all other powers and authorities. Gone are protections for the unborn; gone is the authority of parents over their children; gone are all societal institutions and constraints rooted in a biblical ethic. And gone is any connection or sense of accountability to God.

Socialism is the gatekeeper of a world gone mad. It stands at the city gates granting admission to every perversion of the human heart, while denying the thing we need most—a visitation of the Living God.

And apart from that visitation, life under socialism remains exceptionally uninviting, even dangerous.

A GRIM HISTORY

In his book *Leviathan*, English philosopher and historian Thomas Hobbes wrote about the need for strong central government. He described life without such "security" using an extended litany of woe, and he concluded with these words: "And the life of man: solitary, poor, nasty, brutish, and short."[97]

Hobbes was likely correct as far as he went. But as American journalist and economist Henry Hazlitt says elsewhere in this volume, he did not go far enough in considering the secondary consequences of a strong centralized government. And if Hobbes could have seen the face of the major socialist governments of the 20th century, he might have described them with some of the same rhetoric: nasty, brutish, and with the lives of its citizens being decidedly short.

Indeed, when considering how truly socialist governments "care" for their own citizens, merely being nasty and brutish would be an enormous qualitative improvement. Consider the "democide" that took place in the 20th century alone.

Democide is the term revived and redefined by political scientist R.J. Rummel,[98] and it describes "the murder of any person or people *by their government*, including genocide, politicide, and mass murder" [emphasis added]. Democide would also include deaths resulting from an "intentionally or knowingly reckless and depraved disregard for life," according to Rummel. The mass starvation by Stalin of 7 million Ukrainians in the early 1930s [99] would be a notable example.

In the period 1900-1987, Rummel calculates that 109 million citizens were murdered by their *socialist governments*.[100] Read those last two words again: "socialist governments." This does not include any deaths by war, and specifically excludes the brutal genocides of Germany, Japan, and Turkey.

FAILURE BATHED IN BLOOD

Anyone not troubled by this indisputable record of democide—perhaps the best-established fact of socialism—has a heart a few sizes too small. Remember that every one of those 109 million people had a face—and a mother and a father.

Even if one could successfully argue that socialism works (spoiler alert: it doesn't), social progress measured in blood is anathema. As Roman Catholic cleric and writer Richard John Neuhaus put it: "Progress without the reasoned freedom to think and act is regression to slavery." Even the most obtuse would admit that death (or the threat of it) is a categorical impediment to the freedom to think and act.

This is the true face of totalitarian socialism—a grim reaper, ready (and even eager) to sacrifice its citizens on the failed altar of state power.[101]

SOCIALISM AND THE YOUNG

This reality, of socialist governments murdering their own citizens, stands in stark contrast to the far-more-soothing narrative that captivates sophomores[102] and other voters with a wavering grasp of history.

In some measure, we can understand the naïveté of the young. In our time, they often live a sheltered existence. Their education (at least respecting socialism) often resembles little more than indoctrination.[103] In general, they haven't been taught how to think, only how to feel. And along comes socialism, singing their song—a song of pathos rather than ethos. And the secular culture—particularly the entertainment culture—is creatively lazy on this subject. There are few things more predictable in life than a Hollywood movie with the "bad guy" being a wealthy, corrupt businessman—or a military leader or preacher for that matter.

But this begs a more direct question: Why do young people like socialism so much more than older people do?

Longitudinal research by the Pew Research Trust[104] shows little change in attitudes about socialism over time, with 60 percent of the general population having an unfavorable view of socialism, but with 49 percent of those ages 18 to 29 having a favorable view. A more recent study by the market research firm YouGov found 36 percent of those ages 18 to 29 had a positive view of socialism.[105]

Reporter Sam Sanders at NPR tried to answer the question more heuristically in an *All Things Considered* story.[106] He spoke with students at George Mason University in Northern Virginia. Some, he said, liked the idea of socialism in theory, but less so in practice. Others indicated their view would likely change over time with different life experiences. Yet many still expressed an overall positive view of socialism.

In other conversations with researchers regarding a demographically oriented fascination with socialism, Sanders uncovered two recurring themes: the economy and the perception of European nations with socialist tendencies.

It is true that many young people leaving college in the last eight years have struggled with the lasting effects of what many call the Great Recession. On average these young people seem to be doing less well than their parents at the same age, with lower paying jobs and greater personal debt (much of it in the form of student loans). With their limited, and somewhat unfavorable, experience as their guide, this generation tends to view capitalism less positively.

And when their untrained eyes fall on certain northern European nations noted for their expansive social welfare programs, they tend to see them as empirical support for the viability of socialism.

These northern European nations (largely Scandinavian) are in reality mixed economies. While putatively free market economies, their high rates of taxation and public sector dominated economies tend to impede capital formation. Yet their high levels of public sector employment and expensive social welfare programs do have a socialist bent.[107]

Even so, many economists have long placed these same northern European countries on a financial watch list for their dramatically aging populations and deep dependence on oil revenues. With bloated global oil inventories resulting in a collapse of oil prices and revenues, many of these nations now find that world oil prices are below their actual costs of production. With these global "headwinds," it seems unlikely that the semi-socialist economies of Denmark, Norway, and Sweden will remain unscathed.[108]

It is worth remembering also that it took 70 years for the Soviet Union to collapse. Before young people assume a socialist economic success in northern Europe, it might be best to consider the time horizon. Also it might be worth examining the non-oil, socialist economies of Europe. Greece, anyone?

What Is the Meaning of This?

In their consideration of the youthful bias toward socialism, the folks at *Reason.Org* asked another question: Do young people even know what socialism means?

Based on their *Spring 2014 Millennial Poll*,[109] the answer is "perhaps not." When the *Reason* survey used the term "government-managed economy" (a term, we should note, that is far less radically interventionist than "socialism"), favorable support among millennials dropped from 42 percent to 32 percent. Correspondingly, when the terminology is switched from "capitalism" to "free market economy," favorable support among millennials rises from 52 percent to 64 percent.

In other words, when language about socialism and capitalism are vague, millennials have greater difficulty in expressing a clear viewpoint. This explains a CBS/New York Times survey, showing that when Americans are asked to describe "socialism" in their own words, millennials are least able to do so, with only 16 percent articulating some variation of government ownership or control.[110]

As Emily Ekins at *Reason.Org* explains:

> *Millennials simply don't know that socialism means the government owning everybody's businesses. They don't understand that socialism means the government owns the banks, the car companies, Uber, Apple, Facebook, Amazon, etc. They don't even want the government taking a managerial role over the economy, let alone nationalizing private enterprise.*[111]

SOCIALISM AS A BRAND

If some support for socialism among millennials is the result of lexical difficulties, it is far more difficult to explain away another aspect of the millennial endearment with socialism: its helpful brand positioning in the marketplace of ideas.

Now, with all the negative realities detailed above, how can we argue that socialism has favorable brand awareness? Well, perhaps socialism itself does not. But it stands in the shadow of one of the most powerful brands among millennials: the green movement.

In what political pundit Charles Krauthammer calls a "brilliant gambit,"[112] socialists made an astonishingly adroit pivot: a metamorphosis from red to green. No longer raising the specter of all things red (e.g. Mao, Khmer Rouge, Castro, et al.), the banner of environmentalism now flies above the citadel of socialism. Contemporary culture would call this socialism reinventing itself.

Krauthammer puts it this way:

> *The cultural elites went straight from the memorial service for socialism to the altar of the environment. The objective is the same: highly centralized power given to the best and the brightest, the new class of experts, managers and technocrats. This time, however, the alleged justification is not abolishing oppression and inequality but saving the planet.*

In this way, socialism becomes more acceptable to the young, as the means to a perceived greater good. For them support for socialism becomes almost an exercise in youthful *noblesse oblige*. "I am not like these grasping capitalists, you see; I care." And so on. Never mind that millennials are themselves expert in grasping and consuming every social benefit available (all paid by others) and have shown a readiness to walk away from their own social obligations (e.g. witness the growing default rate on student debt).

So there it is. Just when you thought it was over, socialism is reborn in the garb of radical environmentalism, of which so-called climate change is merely an adornment. As a friend of mine likes to say: "It's like a watermelon: green on the outside, red on the inside."

IMPORTANT KEYS TO SOCIALISM

We must understand that while the premises of socialism are false, the promises it makes will always sound like the right answer. This is so because the problems socialism highlights (and promises to solve) are common to us all. Who does not want more security against the vicissitudes of life? Who does not want guarantees instead of uncertainties? What college student would not want free (to him) tuition? What worker would not want more money for the same work? Who does not want something that appears to cost you nothing? Yet as French political economist Frederic Bastiat memorably put it:

*The state is that great fiction by which everyone tries
to live at the expense of everyone else.*[113]

So the first thing we must remember about socialism is that it fails everywhere it is tried. The only variable in its failure is the time frame of its demise.

A second thing critically important to remember about socialism is its absence of any moral foundation. Without any moral or ethical constraints, socialists tend to be pathologically mendacious. Their lies flow off their lips with ease, because they believe that any lie advancing the cause of socialism is "truth." So they will point to the blue sky and say: "Isn't it awful how green the sky has become? We must do something about that." And they will stare you in the face and propose themselves as the solution.

Nothing brings this home more clearly than the full quote from National Socialist Joseph Goebbels, referenced earlier:

*If you tell a lie big enough and keep repeating it,
people will eventually come to believe it. The lie can
be maintained only for such time as the State can
shield the people from the political, economic and/
or military consequences of the lie. It thus becomes
vitally important for the State to use all of its powers
to repress dissent, for the truth is the mortal enemy
of the lie, and thus by extension, the truth is the
greatest enemy of the State.* [114]

And German philosopher and cultural critic Friedrich Nietzsche puts it more personally with his riposte:

*I am not upset with you because you lied to me. I'm
upset that from now on I can't believe you.*[115]

WHAT WE MUST REMEMBER ABOUT SOCIALISM

So what are the important things to remember about socialism? At least these three:

The Heart of Socialism is Atheistic

Socialism begins with a profoundly belligerent atheism, but is not without "religious" zeal. As Richard John Neuhaus once said: "Socialism is the religion people get when they lose their religion." With atheism as its first defining characteristic, socialism will tolerate no objective moral code.

With no moral compass, socialist societies are everywhere marked by moral decay—and with idolatry. Chief among socialism's idolatrous afflictions is its declaration that "man is the measure of all things." But the harsh reality is that socialism only makes *some* men the measure of all things—its leaders. Socialism is democratic in name only (DINO).

Oddly, in light of its virulent atheism, some Christians are drawn to socialism's stated goal of elevating the common man and helping those who are less fortunate. Some even buy into the argument that Acts chapter five demonstrates the Bible's support for socialism.

But the Bible does not teach socialism. All of it exhortations to help the poor, the widow, and the orphan are directed to us *as individuals*, not offered as a pattern for human government. In fact the narrative of Acts chapter five itself, while presenting persecuted believers holding all their goods in common for the benefit of all, shows them doing it *as private individuals*—not as a government taxing one group for the benefit of another. As pastor and theologian D. James Kennedy says:

I can think of nothing more perfectly designed to give Karl Marx apoplexy than the idea that people should sell all their property and give the money to the church. If there is anything antithetical to the whole spirit of modern socialism it is precisely that. And yet, people have the incredible temerity to say that this passage in Acts teaches modern state socialism. Nothing, indeed, can be farther from the truth.[116]

The Lifeblood of Socialism is Power

After its atheism, socialism's second defining characteristic is its unrelenting drive for power—supreme power, power at all costs. Socialism's principal means of expanding its power is two-fold: 1) by inventing or magnifying problems solely in order to propose solutions that increase its power and control, and 2) by creating dependency.

Seen through this lens, socialism's fascination with the green movement and the global-warming franchise is really only a means to greater power and greater control over the economy, over human activity, and over your money. In like manner, socialism's core values of state ownership of all productive assets, systematic wealth transfers, and preferential funding are all aimed at the same targets: destroying personal initiative and creating dependency on the state—which makes idolaters of all who bow before the state as their provider.

The Advancement of Socialism Destroys Freedom

In the process of fostering dependency, socialism becomes the great destroyer. It destroys wealth and dignity, along with faith, family, and freedom. In the Communist Manifesto[117] Marx and Engels advocated the abolition of the family. In such a state of categorical dependency on government, rights become transitory and circumstantial, not unalienable—freedoms become discretionary, not endowed by our Creator.

Socialism has a definitive record of wretched failure, wherever it is fully tried (North Sea oil, notwithstanding). This is true because socialism is just a giant jobs program for supporters of big government. Witness the so-called War on Poverty. Precious little of the billions spent over the years actually reached the poor. It did, however, create hundreds of thousands of government jobs—to help the poor, you see. And this massive expansion of government employment resulted in an even further bloated bureaucracy—administratively incompetent and all *dependent* upon big government.

Most troubling is the socialist state's aim to crush the human spirit. Socialist governments see such destruction as a necessary bulwark against uprising—whether electoral or otherwise. So we see a transition from dependency to oppression, with diehard socialists ever ready to spill the blood of dissenters. Even as I write these words I am struck by how incongruous they will seem to some. But let me call you back to our earlier discussion of the research of Professor R.J. Rummel, who found that socialist governments murdered 109 million *of their own citizens* in the 20th century alone.

WHAT WE MUST DO ABOUT SOCIALISM

Finding the road back to sanity begins with recognizing that the high priests of socialism who offer the temptations of statist programs and benefits do not seek your welfare. They seek only to bind you to the state, ensuring your dependency. They will not protect and preserve your freedom. They will dictate a politically correct prescription of "rights" while denying fundamental freedoms.

What We Must Do Personally

1. We must flee dependency on government.

2. We must abhor personal debt as a gateway to dependency.

3. We must form small voluntary associations helping others avoid dependency.

4. We must support organizations defending freedom.

5. We must bear witness to Christ as our only hope.

What We Must Do Politically

1. We must define terms carefully. Words matter—we must call socialism what it is. Both modern liberalism and progressivism are just socialism in a bad disguise.

2. We must unmask socialism. The green movement and the global warming franchise are both false fronts for socialism, even if those involved do not fully understand or acknowledge it.

3. We must use words that work. "Free market economy" is more helpfully descriptive than "capitalism." Better than using "socialism" is the phrase "government owned and controlled."

4. We must not vote for candidates promising to expand our benefits.

5. We must starve the socialist beast with tax cuts, supporting those who will do so.

6. We must demand that all taxes be indexed for inflation, which is the greatest economic factor fostering dependency.

7. The central political principle of socialism is that "socialists should be in charge." Therefore, we must beware of those whose primary motivation is that *they* be in charge.

We must do our part, but in the end we can be confident that socialism will run up against Stein's Law, which says: "If something cannot go on forever, it will stop." As Margaret Thatcher put it more practically: "The problem with socialism is that you eventually run out of other people's money."

Communism [Marxist socialism] is neither an economic nor a political system—it is a form of insanity—a temporary aberration which will one day disappear from the Earth because it is contrary to human nature. I wonder how much more misery it will cause before it disappears? [118]

(President Ronald Reagan)

CHAPTER FOUR

THE GREAT CONFUSION
The Insanity of Preferential Gender Identity

So God created man in His own image;
in the image of God He created him;
male and female He created them.

(Genesis 1:27)

A woman must not wear man's clothing,
nor is a man to put on a woman's clothing.
For all that do so are abominations to the
Lord your God.

(Deuteronomy 22:5)

Most shockingly, [the transgendered]
suicide mortality rose almost 20-fold above the
comparable non-transgender population.[119]

(Former Johns Hopkins Hospital psychiatrist-in-chief Paul R. McHugh, M.D.)

"Imagine you're a man. You think everything about you looks like a man should look. You have short hair and a little scruff on your face. When you were born, the doctors said, 'It's a boy!' and that's how your parents raised you. You've always shopped for guys' clothes and no one has ever called you anything other than a boy, guy, dude, or man. Then one day at a restaurant, the waiter asks you, 'Can I get you anything to drink, ma'am?'"

Authors Debby Herbenick and Aleta Baldwin[120] offer this scenario as an aid in imagining what it might feel like to be "perceived" as having a gender other than your own. And that is the world in which we now live—one where perception attempts to create its own reality.

THE MAN IN THE MIRROR

That was the conflicting self-perception of Nick Meinzer, a hairdresser from Oakland, California:

> *From my earliest days I remember feeling uncom-*
> *fortable in my own skin. I was raised by liberal*
> *feminist NYC-living parents in the 70's who did not*
> *believe in gender roles. So I'm very clear from the*
> *get-go, I had no gender roles that dictated there was*
> *something wrong with a girl liking the things I liked.*
> *Yet I just couldn't get over the fact that I knew I was*
> *a boy. As I got older, my body developed at a young*
> *age and I remember and always feeling disconnect-*
> *ed from it, resenting its betrayal in presenting me*
> *incorrectly. In my dreams I was always male, in my*
> *waking hours my hourglass figure was something I*
> *hid, because it felt more like a costume.* [121]

Of all the indicators pointing to our cultural disconnect from truth, the astonishing emergence of perplexing and confusing notions of gender identity is perhaps the most profound. Nowhere is mankind's separation from the Creator more evident than in this headlong flight from biological reality.

LOGICAL DIFFICULTIES

Gender identities in our day have become legion. And this multiplicity of identities seems (to most people) detached from any rational notion of human existence.

On its face, the idea of gender divorced from the inescapable reality of DNA seems a failure in logic above all else. Call yourself what you will, your chromosomes rise before the Judge with an irrefutable objection.

The second logical challenge for those trying to make sense of the transgender landscape is the inconstancy of gender ID. Those who claim a gender ID other than their biological one also avow the right to change back if they wish—or to change to some third or fourth identity based upon any whim whatsoever. For example, if a transgender woman argues that her female chromosomal identity assigned at conception is not the essence of who she is, all that is needed is to declare a new gender ID, with the full expectation that others will at least respect her decision. And if she later changes her mind, so be it.

A DEFINITIONAL CONUNDRUM

Perhaps most emblematic of the definitional difficulties faced even by those sympathetic to the gender ID conundrum is Facebook's efforts to be gender-friendly in accommodating its users. Beginning with a list of 51 possible gender identities (later increased to 70), Facebook leadership raised a responsive "white flag" with this administrative posting:

Facebook Diversity [122]
Last year we were proud to add a custom gender

option to help people better express their identities on Facebook. We collaborated with our Network of Support, a group of leading LGBT advocacy organizations, to offer an extensive list of gender identities that many people use to describe themselves. After a year of offering this feature, we have expanded it to include a free-form field. Now, if you do not identify with the pre-populated list of gender identities, you are able to add your own. **As before, you can add up to ten gender terms and also have the ability to control the audience with whom you would like to share your custom gender.** *We recognize that some people face challenges sharing their true gender identity with others, and this setting gives people the ability to express themselves in an authentic way. The expanded custom gender option is available to everyone who uses Facebook in US English* [emphasis added].

MANIFOLD CONFUSION

For those wondering how there could be 70 (or more) gender identities, and what the descriptive labels mean, here is an extensive listing [123] with some definitions—from a transgender perspective:

Agender:
This is someone who does not identify with any sort of gender identity. Someone who intentionally has no recognizable gender presentation may also use this term. Some people use similar terms such as "genderless" and "gender neutral."

Androgyne/androgynous:
This is someone who neither identifies with, nor presents as, a man or woman. Androgynous can refer to having both masculine and feminine qualities. This term has Latin roots: *andro,* meaning "man" and *gyne,* meaning "woman." Some androgynes may

identify as "gender benders," meaning that they are intentionally "bending" (or challenging) societal gender roles.

Bigender:

This is someone who identifies as both a man and a woman. A Bigender identity is a combination of these two genders, but not necessarily a 50/50 combination, as these genders are often felt—and expressed—fully. Similar to individuals who identify as gender fluid, bigender people may present as men, as women, or as gender-neutral ways on different days.

Cis:

All of these terms (with the prefix "cis") capture that a person is not trans or does not have a gender diverse identity or presentation. Cis Female (see also Cis Woman, Cisgender Female, Cisgender Woman) is a female who identifies as a woman and has a feminine gender identity. Cis Male (see also Cis Man, Cisgender Male, Cisgender Man) is a male who identifies as a man having a masculine gender identity.

Female to Male / F2M / FTM:

A trans person who was assigned female sex and now lives as a man and has a masculine gender identity. This person may or may not have altered her physical body with surgery, hormones, or other modifications (e.g., voice training to develop a deeper spoken voice). FTM is an abbreviation of female to male. Generally uses masculine pronouns (e.g., "he" or "his") or gender-neutral pronouns.

Gender Fluid:

This is someone whose gender identity and presentation are not confined to only one gender category. Gender fluid people may have dynamic or fluctuating understandings of their gender, moving between categories as feels right. For example, a gender fluid person might feel more like a man one day and more like a woman on another day, or that neither term is a good fit.

Gender Non-conforming:

Someone who looks and/or behaves in ways that do not conform to, or are atypical of, society's expectations of how a person of that gender should look or behave.

Gender Questioning:

This is someone who may be questioning their gender or gender identity, and/or considering other ways of experiencing or expressing their gender or gender presentation.

Genderqueer:

Someone who identifies outside of, or wishes to challenge, the two-gender system, or who may identify as multiple genders, a combination of genders, or "between" genders. People who use this term may feel they are reclaiming the word "queer", which has historically been used as a slur against gay men and women. This term is used more often by younger generations doing the "reclaiming" and less often by slightly older generations who may have personally experienced the term "queer" as a slur.

Hermaphrodite / Intersex:

This generally refers to someone whose chromosomes, gonads (i.e., ovaries or testes), hormonal profiles, and anatomy do not conform to the expected configurations of either male-typical or female-typical bodies. Some intersex conditions are apparent at birth, while others are noticed around puberty or later. Some individuals no longer use the term "intersex conditions" and instead prefer "disorders of sex development."

Male to Female / M2F / MTF:

A trans person who was assigned male sex and now lives as a woman and has a feminine gender identity. This person may or may not have altered his physical body with surgery, hormones, or other modification (e.g., voice training, electrolysis, etc.). MTF is an abbreviation of "Male To Female." Generally uses female pronouns (e.g., "she" or "her") or gender-neutral pronouns.

Neither:

Chooses not to put a label on one's gender.

Neutrois:

This is an umbrella term within the bigger umbrella terms of transgender or genderqueer. Includes people who do not identify within the binary gender system (i.e., man/woman).

Non-binary:

Similar to genderqueer, this is a way of describing one's gender as outside the two-gender (i.e., man/woman) system and/or challenging that system.

Other:

Choosing to not provide a commonly recognized label to one's gender. When used by those describing themselves, this may feel like a freeing way of describing (or not specifically describing) their gender. The term "other" should not be used to refer to people whose gender you can't quite understand or place.

Pangender:

"Pan" means every (or all), and this is another identity label such as genderqueer or neutrois that challenges binary gender and is inclusive of gender diverse people.

Trans:

This is an inclusive term, referring to the many ways one can transcend or even transgress gender or gender norms (e.g., it includes individuals who may identify as transgender, transsexual, gender diverse, etc.). In many cases the asterisk (*) is not followed by a sex or gender term—it's just written as "Trans*" to indicate that not all trans people identify with an established sex or gender label.

Transgender:

An umbrella term that includes all people who have genders not traditionally associated with their assigned sex. People who identify as transgender may, or may not, have altered their bodies through surgery and/or hormones. Some examples: Trans Man (see FTM above). Although some people write the term as "transman" (no space between trans and man) or trans-man (note the hyphen), some advocate for a space to be included between "trans" and "man" in order to indicate that the person is a man and that the "trans" part may not be a defining characteristic or central to his identity. Trans Woman (see MTF above). Although some people write the term as "transwoman" (no space between trans and woman) or trans-woman (note the hyphen), some advocate for a space to be included between "trans" and "woman" in order to indicate that the person is a woman and that the "trans" part may not be a defining characteristic or central to her identity.

Trans Person:

Another way of saying someone is a transgender person (see above). (Note: "transgender" tends to be preferred over "transgendered").

Transsexual Man:

This is someone who was assigned female at birth who has most likely transitioned (such as through surgery and/or hormones) to living as a man.

Transsexual Person:

For many people this term indicates that a person has made lasting changes to their physical body, specifically their sexual anatomy (e.g., genitals and/or breasts or chest), through surgery. For some, the term "transsexual" is a problematic term because of its history of pathology or association with a psychological disorder. In order to get the operations necessary for sexual reassignment surgeries or gender confirming surgeries, people long needed a psychiatric diagnosis (historically, that diagnosis was called "transsexualism") and recommendations from mental health professionals. The term "transsexual" tends to be used less often by younger generations of trans persons.

Transsexual Woman:

This is someone who was assigned male sex at birth who has most likely transitioned (such as through surgery and/or hormones) to living as a woman. (Bruce "Caitlin" Jenner would be a contemporary example.)

Transfeminine:

Someone assigned a male sex at birth and who identifies as feminine, but may not identify wholly as a woman. Often you will encounter the phrase "feminine of center" to indicate where people who identify as transfeminine see themselves in relation to other genders.

Transmasculine:

Someone assigned a female sex at birth and who identifies as masculine, but may not identify wholly as a man. Often you will encounter the phrase "masculine of center" to indicate where people who identify as transmasculine see themselves in relation to other genders.

Two-spirit:

This term likely originated with the Zuni tribe of North America, though two-spirit persons have been documented in numerous tribes. Native Americans, who have both masculine and feminine characteristics and presentations, have distinct roles in their tribes, and they are seen as a third gender.

Additional preferred transgender descriptors:

Asexual	*T* Man*
Cis Female	*T* Woman*
Cis Male	*Trans Female*
Cis Man	*Trans Male*
Cis Woman	*Trans Man*
Cisgender	*Trans Woman*
Cisgender Female	*Trans*Female*
Cisgender Male	*Trans*Male*
Cisgender Man	*Trans*Man*
Cisgender Woman	*Trans*Person*
Female to Male	*Trans*Woman*
Female to male trans man	*Transsexual*
Female to male transgender man	*Transsexual Female*
Female to male transsexual man	*Transsexual Male*
Intersex Man	*Transgender Male*
Intersex Person	*Transgender Man*
Intersex Woman	*Transgender Female*
Male to female trans woman	*Transgender Person*
Male to female transgender woman	*Transgender Woman*
Male to female transsexual woman	*Two-spirit person*
Man	*Two* person*
Polygender	*Woman*

WHY SO MANY DESCRIPTORS?

While even a cursory review of this list and its definitions reveals significant redundancies and sometimes minor definitional tweaks to suit personal preferences, this wide array of choices is in keeping with the *preferential* versus *existential* nature of gender identity.

What matters most is to define oneself. In important ways, gender identity is not really about who you are—or even about how others see you. Gender identity is largely about demanding that others see you as you *wish* to be seen.

But this demand to be recognized as you wish gets even more complicated, even mystifying, when you consider two additional implications of these wide-ranging gender identities.

WHO SAID I HAVE ONLY ONE IDENTITY?

First, let me recall your attention to the Facebook administrative posting on gender identities reprinted above. In the middle of Facebook's explanation of the new custom gender category is this sentence:

> *As before, you can add up to **ten gender terms** and also have the ability to control the audience with whom you would like to share your custom gender.*

So we go from watching confused people demanding to be recognized as they wish, to people wanting to have multiple (up to ten!) gender identities. This is exponential confusion. But wait (as the commercial says) it gets even more complicated.

THIS IS MY IDENTITY TODAY . . .

Second, note that one of the gender descriptors detailed above provides an important clue to another contemporary gender concept. I am referring to the term: *Gender Fluid*. And here is the definition from the list above:

> *Gender Fluid: Someone whose gender identity and presentation are not confined to only one gender category. Gender fluid people may have dynamic or*

fluctuating understandings of their gender, moving between categories as feels right. For example, a gender fluid person might feel more like a man one day and more like a woman on another day, or that neither term is a good fit.

When in Rome

Consider Rhonda Williams, a systems engineer and writer from West Palm Beach, Florida:

I have spent a significant amount of [my] life questioning my gender identity and do not fit into the binary male/female continuum. I view this [the] same, as I am right handed, blue eyed, and dyslexic. I have not made it an issue.

Born in the wrong body is how some transgender or gender variant individuals might describe themselves. Nevertheless, which body is wrong for me? Neither. I am not confined or conflicted and comfortable as both.

I am both genders psychologically and always have been. I take both roles seriously, being the best person that I can be. I am an individual who can be more or less masculine and more or less feminine as my frame of mind and circumstances allow. I think that is true of everyone, but a few, like myself, exhibit this greater prerequisite and range. In computer terms— my operating system is flexible.[124]

Rhonda's story exemplifies one of the implicit demands of the transgender population—that changing one's gender identity (at any time and for any reason) is perfectly acceptable. But (and here is where the insanity is magnified even further) embedded within the concept of gender fluidity is the notion that society must stand ready to accept and fully accommodate everyone riding this see-saw of what looks to some more like gender schizophrenia.

If I want to be a man today using the boys bathroom, and be a woman tomorrow using the girls bathroom, and be something else the third day, well, you just need to deal with it! And here is where the truth about the LGBT rights movement comes home to roost.

For many in the transgender movement, it has never been about tolerance. It is about forcing others to both accept and celebrate their choices. If you don't think so, try calling Caitlin Jenner by his given name: Bruce.

A Princess Boy

This forced celebration is sometimes masked as accommodation, which was the experience of a *kindergarten class* at the Nova Classical Academy, a charter school in Minnesota. Parents were informed via email from the elementary school principal that in the coming days, the school would be taking steps to "support a student who is gender nonconforming." These five- and six-year-old children, according to the email, "will listen to various books that celebrate differences and will be teaching children about the beauty of being themselves." One of those books titled "A Princess Boy" is the story of a boy who sometimes likes to do "traditional girl things like wear dresses."[125]

Many parents were naturally concerned about whether the subject was age-appropriate for kindergartners. One mother of a six-year-old girl said:

> *If physiologists and medical doctors don't quite understand gender fluidity, then why do we try to impose this on people who are just trying to figure out how to tie their shoe?* [126]

In the end, ten children transferred to other schools, and school administrators report that for the first time in Nova Classical Academy's 12-year history, applications were down significantly.

SUBJECTIVITY VS. RATIONALISM

It is well worth noting that this capricious aspect of gender identity is a revolutionary development and a departure of notions of gender identity from as little as ten years ago. Prior to the emergence of seemingly impulsive and erratic notions of gender identity, a self-declaration of gender followed a pattern.

The logical case went like this: People would argue that while conceived as "A" they are really "B." In fact they knew they were "B" from a very young age, and they are quite confident that God intended them to live as "B." (Poor God; He must have gotten confused in mismatching their chromosomes and their essential identity).

While hard to fathom existentially, there is at least a logical argument here, in that such people are persuaded their gender identity is different than their biological identity. Yet in more recent years, even such awkward logic is absent. The argument is no longer *existential*. Instead it has become solely *preferential*.

THE NEO-GENDER ARGUMENT

The contemporary gender identity argument goes like this: While my DNA declares me to be "A," I simply *prefer* to be "B"— or whatever else I choose to be. Thus, I no longer have a gender identity rooted in any objective reality. Once again paraphrasing the Cheshire Cat: "When you don't know where you are going, any road will take you there."

One can almost hear the echoes of the poem *Invictus*, birthed in the Garden of Eden and later penned by English poet, Ernest Henley:

Out of the night that covers me,
Black as the pit from pole to pole,
I thank whatever gods may be
For my unconquerable soul.

In the fell clutch of circumstance
I have not winced nor cried aloud.
Under the bludgeonings of chance
My head is bloody, but unbowed.

Beyond this place of wrath and tears
Looms but the Horror of the shade,
And yet the menace of the years
Finds and shall find me unafraid.

It matters not how strait the gate,
How charged with punishments the scroll,
I am the master of my fate,
I am the captain of my soul.

But this is one lonely captain.

A RADICAL ABANDONMENT

In this radical shift from the existential to the preferential, there is something profound that we dare not miss. By abandoning the existential argument few seem to realize that this neo-gender approach of subjective and capricious choice completely undermines the first principle of most homosexual dogma: *that God made me this way.*

Of course, the argument that "God made them this way" is not a biblical argument. The Bible is clear, rather, that in their sin and the hardening of their hearts, God "gave them over" to do that which should not be done. Yet in abandoning any notion that one's existence is shaped by the will of God, the only alternative is adopting the Prime Directive of secularism: The choice is mine—any choice, any time. Sadly for transgender advocates, because of this capricious reasoning, even many sympathetic observers find it exceedingly difficult to take them seriously.

IMPORTANT KEYS TO GENDER IDENTITY

It's a Matter of Choice

Many people believe being transgender is a matter of sexual orientation—as in "I was made this way." But in the main, gender identity is seen as a matter of choice—as in "this is who I choose to be."

It's a Matter of Self-Definition

But if choice is foundational to gender identity, it's defining characteristic is self-definition. It is not a binary choice: male or female. It is a defining choice. It is the choice to define oneself as one wishes to be known. Proof positive of self-defining nature of gender identity is the more than 70 gender identities collected by Facebook, allowing everyone a custom definition.

It's a Matter of Fluidity

If the defining characteristics of gender identity are choice and self-definition, the close corollary is that any choice made might be transitive and fluid. This is the demand that no one is bound by a single identity over time. This notion is dramatically at variance with any prior conception of gender identity, where people would argue that their *essential* identity was B, even if their biological identity was A.

It's a Matter of Expectation

And all of these aspects of gender identity (choice, self-definition, and fluidity) are bound up in the irrational expectation that society must provide accommodation, even if one has a different gender identity for every day of the week.

WHAT WE MUST REMEMBER ABOUT GENDER INDENTITY

As frustrating and seeming irrational as all these things are, we must have compassion for the brokenhearted. At base, the story of those who are transgender is one of sexual brokenness. Yes, it is also rebellion. But all who now look to Christ in faith were once rebels also. As Paul writes to the church at Corinth:

> *Do you not know that the unrighteous will not inherit the kingdom of God? Do not be deceived. Neither the sexually immoral, nor idolators, nor adulterers, nor male prostitutes, nor homosexuals, nor thieves, nor covetous, nor drunkards, nor revilers, nor extortioners will inherit the kingdom of God.* **_But such were some of you._** *But you were washed, you were sanctified, and you were justified in the name of the Lord Jesus by the Spirit of our God* (1 Corinthians 6:9-11) [emphasis added].

If you have no compassion for the transgendered, it may be because you do not know their stories. They are heartbreaking. Their lives often go from rejection to confusion, from confusion to anger, from anger to dysphoria, and too often from dysphoria to death. They have an extraordinarily high rate of suicide. They, too, need the healing that can be found only in Jesus.

WHAT WE MUST DO ABOUT GENDER IDENTITY

Our compassion for the sexually broken must be genuine—as the Apostle said: "such were some of you." But true compassion does not obviate the need for common sense and a biblical perspective, which requires at least five things:

1. Recognition that the transgendered have the same civil rights as all citizens

We must gratefully acknowledge that all people have the same civil rights, which should and must be respected.

2. Recognition that the transgendered have civil rights, not special rights

While all people have the same civil rights, the civil rights of transgender people are not superior to the rights of others.

3. Recognition that children are at risk in this confusion

The American College of Pediatricians has warned educators and legislators that "conditioning children into believing a lifetime of chemical and surgical impersonation of the opposite sex is normal and healthful is child abuse." In a published statement the doctors argue that "a person's belief that he or she is something they are not is, at best, a sign of confused thinking."[127]

4. Recognition that we bring judgment on ourselves if we do not protect children

We must defend children even to the point of civil disobedience. This issue of allowing the transgender to pick the boy's restroom today and the girl's restroom tomorrow cannot stand. Given the stated LGBT goal of recruiting the young, they cannot be trusted with the best interests of children.[128] A reasonable accommodation should be made—but one that does not involve a biological male entering places where biological females are vulnerable, or vice versa.

5. Recognition that elected officials must look to the interests of children first

Any elected official unwilling to put the interests of children first, in these circumstances, should be singled out as an enabler of sin and potentially an abuser of children.

In Search of Hope

While we must stand against the insanity of the gender identity antagonists, we dare not forget that the transgender people among us are lost, broken, and looking for hope. While that hope is found only in Christ, those who remember that the undeserving grace of God came to us "while we were yet sinners" can communicate that grace best. Jesus praised those who would give a cup of cold water in His name. How much more will He praise those who are willing to extend a loving cup of hope to those who desperately need it?

In his book, *Love Hunger: A Harrowing Journey from Sexual Addiction to True Fulfillment*, David Kyle Foster unpacks a life of rejection, characterized by desperate loneliness and sexual brokenness. But in his descent to the bondage of homosexuality, prostitution, and pornography, David discovers, like many before him, that he is never beyond the reach of Jesus' love.

Listen to David's own words:

> *I never expected to live this long . . . I have been an expert in rebellion against God . . .*
>
> *I know sexual brokenness . . . I know bondage and addiction . . . I know the unspeakable pain behind*

*intense self-hatred . . . I know the hypocrisy of
religious people . . . I know the poverty and weakness
of self-righteousness.*

*[But] I know the power of God that is able to keep me
from falling. I know the love and grace of God that
has so transformed my heart that I no longer want to
commit the sins that once possessed me. I know the
God who can set <u>anyone</u> free from <u>anything</u> . . . and I
know that God loves you. And He has declared in His
word that anyone who calls on the name of the Lord
Jesus Christ will be saved* [129] [emphasis in original].

To him who overcomes I will give the hidden manna to eat. And I will give him a white stone, and on the stone a new name written, which no one knows except he who receives it.

(Revelation 2:17b)

CONCLUSION

The story of Christian reformation, revival, and renaissance underscores that the darkest hour is often just before the dawn, so we should always be people of hope and prayer, not gloom and defeatism. God the Holy Spirit can turn the situation around in five minutes.[130]

(Author and social critic, Os Guiness)

In the fall of 1863, Abraham Lincoln stood on the battlefield at Gettysburg, nearly five months after 51,000 men died there. Our nation's 16th president then removed his handwritten notes from his vest pocket, and began speaking in a measured cadence. He spoke there about those who gave "the last full measure of their devotion," and he expressed his hope:

> [T]hat this nation, under God, shall have a new birth of freedom—and that government of the people, by the people, and for the people, shall not perish from the Earth.

The horror of that battlefield never left Lincoln. And neither did his sense that the Civil War was God's doing—that it was God's judgment on the entire nation, for both northern factories and southern plantations profited from slavery. But in the end, Lincoln concluded that while slavery was the proximate cause of the war, judgment had come upon the nation for an altogether more significant and historic reason.

Lincoln wrote about this other reason, just three months before the battle at Gettysburg in his *Proclamation Appointing a National Fast Day*, dated March 30, 1863. In it he wrote:

And whereas it is the duty of nations as well as of men, to own their dependence upon the overruling power of God, to confess their sins and transgressions, in humble sorrow, yet with assured hope that genuine repentance will lead to mercy and pardon; and to recognize the sublime truth, announced in the Holy Scriptures and proven by all history, that those nations only are blessed whose God is the Lord.

And, insomuch as we know that, by His divine law, nations like individuals are subjected to punishments and chastisements in this world, may we not justly fear that the awful calamity of civil war, which now desolates the land, may be but a punishment, inflicted upon us, for our presumptuous sins, to the needful end of our national reformation as a whole People? We have been the recipients of the choicest bounties of Heaven. We have been preserved, these many years, in peace and prosperity. We have grown in numbers, wealth and power, as no other nation has ever grown.

But we have forgotten God.

We have forgotten the gracious hand which preserved us in peace, and multiplied and enriched and strengthened us; and we have vainly imagined, in the deceitfulness of our hearts, that all these blessings were produced by some superior wisdom and virtue of our own. Intoxicated with unbroken success, we have become too self-sufficient to feel the necessity of redeeming and preserving grace, too proud to pray to the God that made us!

It behooves us then, to humble ourselves before the offended Power, to confess our national sins, and to pray for clemency and forgiveness.

Lincoln spoke also of the judgment of God in his Second Inaugural Address, delivered on the east steps of the U.S. Capitol Building—not quite 20 months *after* the battle at Gettysburg. These words are cut in marble at the Lincoln Memorial in Washington, D.C. They are on the wall directly opposite the chiseled words of the Gettysburg address. They stand as two great sentinels on either side of the statue of the great man.

In the last portion of this Second Inaugural address, Lincoln grappled with the question of Divine providence. He pondered God's will in allowing such a horrific conflict, marked by the loss of 750,000 lives,[131] with hundreds of thousands more wounded and maimed. Speaking of the people both north and south he said:

> *The Almighty has His own purposes. "Woe unto the world because of offenses; for it must needs be that offenses come, but woe to that man by whom the offense cometh." If we shall suppose that American slavery is one of those offenses which, in the providence of God, must needs come, but which, having continued through His appointed time, He now wills to remove, and that He gives to both North and South this terrible war as the woe due to those by whom the offense came, shall we discern therein any departure from those divine attributes which the believers in a living God always ascribe to Him? Fondly do we hope, fervently do we pray, that this mighty scourge of war may speedily pass away. Yet, if God wills that it continue until all the wealth piled by the bondsman's two hundred and fifty years of unrequited toil shall be sunk, and until every drop of blood drawn with the lash shall be paid by another drawn with the sword, as was said three thousand years ago, so still it must be said "the judgments of the Lord are true and righteous altogether."*

With malice toward none, with charity for all, with firmness in the right as God gives us to see the right, let us strive on to finish the work we are in, to bind up the nation's wounds, to care for him who shall have borne the battle and for his widow and his orphan, to do all which may achieve and cherish a just and lasting peace among ourselves and with all nations.[132]

The Scriptures remind us that the church itself is perpetually at war in the battle for truth. It is for us to proclaim truth to a world that rejects it. It is for us to bear witness to Christ before a watching and listening world—even a world that seems to have declared war on the church. This is the will of God for us in Christ Jesus.

The goal of this brief volume was to examine four byways on our cultural journey where we seem to have lost our way, and to help us to chart a course back to freedom as a nation under God. For us, even if the world has seemingly gone insane, we know that the road back to sanity begins with remembering.

We need to remember the heights from which *we* have fallen. As the church, we need to repent and do the things we did before. These are essentially the same words Jesus spoke to the church at Ephesus in the second chapter of Revelation:

Remember therefore from where you have fallen. Repent, and do the works you did at first, or else I will come to you quickly and remove your candlestick from its place, unless you repent (Revelation 2:5).

The King is coming. And when He comes, may He find us faithful!

ENDNOTES

1. Wikipedia, the free encyclopedia, "Unintended consequences," https://en.wikipedia.org/wiki/Unintended_consequences (accessed March 2016).

2. Mayo Clinic Staff, "Antibiotics: Misuse puts you and others at risk," (December 12, 2014), http://www.mayoclinic.org/healthy-lifestyle/consumer-health/in-depth/antibiotics/art-20045720.

3. Child Trends Data Bank, "Appendix 1—Percentage of all births that were to unmarried women," (December 2015), http://www.childtrends.org/wp-content/uploads/2015/03/75_ appendix1.pdf.

4. Robert Rector, "How the war on poverty was lost," The Wall Street Journal, (January 7, 2014), http://www.wsj.com/news/articles/SB10001424052702303345104579282760272285556.

5. Henry Hazlitt, Economics in One Lesson, (New York: Three Rivers Press, 1946).

6. Bill O'Reilly and Martin Dugard, Killing Reagan, (New York: Henry Holt and Company, 2015), page 209: footnote #1.

7. Marcus Aurelius, translated by Robert Graves, Meditations, (1792).

8. Alasdair MacIntyre, After Virtue: A Study in Moral Theory, 2nd ed., (Notre Dame: University of Notre Dame Press, 1984), 253.

9. Harry S. Truman, "Address Before the Attorney General's Conference on Law Enforcement Problems," (February 15, 1950).

10. Socialist establishmentarian is a self-evident term describing the high priests, viziers, and advocates of the secular socialist state. While chapter three reviews the broad framework of socialism, the malicious tentacles of its reach are seen throughout this discussion.

11. D. James Kennedy and Jerry Newcombe, The Gates of Hell Shall Not Prevail, (Nashville: Thomas Nelson, 1996).

12. Christians do have friends in this battle. Among them are the Alliance Defending Freedom, the American Center for Law and Justice, First Liberty, Liberty Counsel, and the Pacific Justice Institute.

13. The German word schadenfreude captures the sense of having a secret satisfaction derived from the misfortune of others.

14. Sean Higgins, "ACLU fights its own workers' union, complains of 'extortion' tactics," Washington Examiner, (July 31, 2103), http://www.washingtonexaminer.com/aclu-fights-its-own-workers-union-complains-of-extortion-tactics/article/2533764.

15. "The pot calling the kettle black" is an older idiom my father used when pointing out that someone was guilty of the very thing of which they accused another.

16. National Archives, "The Bill of Rights," (accessed March 2016), http://www.archives.gov/exhibits/charters/bill_of_rights_transcript.html.

17. Michael W. McConnell provides an excellent outline of the important issues surrounding establishment. This section relies heavily on his excellent work. Source: Michael W. McConnell, "Establishment and Disestablishment at the Founding, Part I: Establishment of Religion," William & Mary Law Review, (2003),Volume 44, ISSUE 5.

18. Ibid.

19. Ibid.

20. Ibid.

21. H.J. Eckenrode, *Separation of Church and State In Virginia*, (1910).

22. William Waller Hening, *The Statutes at Large Being a Collection of All the Laws in Virginia*, (New York: Bartow, 1823).

23. James Madison, "Letter to William Bradford," (January 24, 1774).

24. Arthur P. Middleton, The Colonial Virginia Parish, History Magazine Protestant Episcopal Church 431, 435-36 (1971).

25. Albert Edward McKinley, *The Suffrage Franchise in the Thirteen English Colonies in America*, (1905).

26. Gerard V. Bradley, "The No Religious Test Clause and the Constitution of Religious Liberty: A Machine That Has Gone of Itself," 37 *Case Western Reserve Law Review* 674, 681 (1987).

27. "Freedom of Religion and the Establishment Clause," *National Paralegal College*, (accessed March 2016), http://nationalparalegal.edu/conLawCrimProc_Public/ FreedomOfExpression/FreedomOfReligion&EstCl.asp.

28. *Everson v. Board of Education*, 330 U.S. 1 (1947).

29. "Everson v. Board of Education of the Township of Ewing," *Oyez*, Chicago-Kent College of Law at Illinois Tech, (accessed March 2016), https://www.oyez.org/cases/1940-1955/330us1.

30. Thomas Jefferson, "Letter to messers. Nehemiah Dodge, Ephraim Robbins, & Stephen S. Nelson, a committee of the Danbury Baptist association in the state of Connecticut," (January 1, 1802).

31. *Everson v. Board of Education*, 330 U.S. 1 (1947).

32. Brief of the American Civil Liberties Union as *Amicus Curiae* at 8, 12, 34.

33. *McCollum v. Board of Education*, 333 U.S. 203 (1948) (Reed, J., dissenting).

34. *Engel v. Vitale*, 370 U.S. 421 (1962) (Stewart, J., dissenting).

35. Mark A. Beliles and Jerry Newcombe, *Doubting Thomas: The Religious Life and Legacy of Thomas Jefferson*, (New York: Morgan James Publishing, 2015).

36. Daniel L. Dreisbach, "The Mythical 'Wall of Separation': How a Misused Metaphor Changed Church–State Law, Policy, and Discourse," *The Heritage Foundation*, (June 23, 2006), http://www.heritage.org/research/reports/2006/06/the-mythical-wall-of-separation-how-a-misused-metaphor-changed-church-state-law-policy-and-discourse.

37. *Newseum Institute*, "Has the Supreme Court defined religion?" (accessed March 2016) http://www.newseuminstitute.org/about/faq/has-the-u-s-supreme-court-defined-religion/.

38. *Torcaso v. Watkins*, 367 U.S. 488 (1961).

39. *Lemon v. Kurtzman*, 403 U.S. 602 (1971).

40. Allen Nevins, *The American States During and After the Revolution*, (New York: MacMillan, 1924).

41. George Mason, "Virginia Declaration of Rights," (1776) Article 16.

42. James Madison, "Remarks: Virginia Ratifying Convention," (June 12, 1788, Papers 11:130—31).

43. Jared Sparks ed., *The Writings of George Washington 12 Volumes*, (Boston: American Stationers Company, 1837).

44. Charles Francis Adams ed., *The Works of John Adams, Second President of the United States*, (Boston: Little, Brown & Co., 1854).

45. Thomas Jefferson, "Second Inaugural Address," (March 4, 1805), The Avalon Project, *Yale Law School*, http://avalon.law.yale.edu/19th_century/jefinau2.asp.

46. Henry P. Johnson ed., *The Correspondence and Public Papers of John Jay*, (New York: Burt Franklin, 1970).

47. John Quincy Adams, "Letter to an autograph collector," (27 April 1837), published in *The Historical Magazine* (July 1860), pp. 193-194. [A variant of the quote was later published in 1860 by John Wingate Thornton, *The Pulpit of The American Revolution*]

48. Daniel Webster, *The Works of Daniel Webster*, (Boston: Little, Brown & Co., 1853).

49. *Zorach v. Clausen*, 343 U.S. 306 307 313 (1952).

50. *Marsh v. Chambers*, 463 U.S. 783 (1983).

51. *Wallace v. Jaffree*, 472 U.S. 38, 107 (1985) (Rehnquist, J., dissenting).

52. Alan Dershowitz, *Rights From Wrongs*, (New York: Basic Books, 2005).

53. In an MSNBC interview, Melinda Henneberger told Chris Matthews: "Maybe the Founders were wrong to guarantee free exercise of religion in the First Amendment, but that is what they did and I don't think we have to choose here," Source: Andrew McCarthy, "WaPo Political Writer: Maybe the Founders were wrong to guarantee the free exercise of religion," *National Review*, (February 10, 2012), http://www. nationalreview.com/corner/290732/wapo-political-writer-maybe-founders-were-wrong-guarantee-free-exercise-religion.

54. James Madison, "Federalist Paper #43," (January 23, 1788),

55. http://www.thefederalistpapers.org/federalist-papers/federalist-paper-43-the-powers-conferred-by-the-constitution-further-considered-continued. This was Thomas Jefferson's main objection to the entire Constitution. In a letter to James Madison Jefferson admitted being disturbed by "the abandonment in every instance of the necessity of rotation in office." Jefferson's experience persuaded him that, in the absence of term limits, every elected official would be "an officer for life." This is exactly what we have in our federal judiciary. Source: Jack Lynch, "One of the Most Intriguing Might-Have-Beens in American History," *Colonial Williamsburg Journal*, (Spring 2007).

56. Augustine of Hippo is the author of the *City of God*, which presents human history dichotomously as a struggle between the City of God (marked by dedication to God's truth) and the earthly City of Man (marked by captivation with the pleasures of the present world). Source: *Wikipedia: The Free Encyclopedia*, "The City of God (book)," (accessed March 2016). https://en.wikipedia.org/wiki/The_City_of_God_(book)

57. *Wallace v. Jaffree*, 472 U.S. 38, 107 (1985) (Rehnquist, J., dissenting).

58. Charles de Secondat, Baron de Montesquieu, *On the Spirit of Laws*, (1748).

59. Peter Barenboim, *Biblical Roots of the Separation of Powers*, (Moscow: Moscow Florentine Society, 2005).

60. Lord John Dahlberg-Acton, "Lord Acton Quote Archive," *Acton Institute for the Study of Religion and Liberty*, (accessed March 2016), http://www.acton.org/research/lord-acton-quote-archive.

61. James Madison, "Speech in the Virginia Ratifying Convention on the Control of the Military," (June 16, 1788).

62. Thomas Jefferson, "Letter to Abigail Adams," (1804). Source: Lipscomb and Bergh, ed., *The Writing of Thomas Jefferson, Memorial Edition*, (Washington, DC, 1903).

63. *Marbury vs. Madison*, 5 U.S. 137 (1803).

64. *Wikipedia: The Free Encyclopedia,* "Usurper," (accessed March 2016), https://en.wikipedia.org/wiki/Usurper.

65. Jonathan Macey, "Executive Branch Usurpation of Power: Corporations and Capital Markets," 115 *Yale Law Journal,* 2416 (2006).

66. Rahm Emanuel, "Comments made at a *Wall Street Journal* conference of corporate chief executives," (November 2008), Source: YouTube Video, (accessed March 2016), https://www.youtube.com/watch?v=1yeA_kHHLow.

67. Abraham Lincoln, *Abraham Lincoln Presidential Library Foundation,* (accessed March 2016), http://www.alplm.org/272viewessay.aspx?id=775.

68. Oath of Office: President of the United States, Heritage Guide to the Constitution, *Heritage Foundation,* (accessed March 2016), http://www.heritage.org/constitution#!/articles/2/essays/85/oath-of-office.

69. Debate Club, "Is President Obama Abusing Executive Power?" *U.S. News & World Report,* (undated), http://www.usnews.com/debate-club/is-president-obama-abusing-executive-power.

70. Ross Douthat, "The making of an Imperial President," *The New York Times,* (November 22, 2014), http://www.nytimes.com/2014/11/23/opinion/sunday/ross-douthat-the-making-of-an-imperial-president.html?_r=0.

71. Jim Eckman, "President Obama and the Separation of Powers," *Issues in Perspective,* (December 27, 2014), https://graceuniversity.edu/iip/2014/12/president-obama-and-the-separation-of-powers/.

72. Rick Moran, "George Will: Stopping a lawless president," *American Thinker,* (June 22, 2014), http://www.americanthinker.com/blog/2014/06/george_will_stopping_a_lawless-president.html.

73. Debate Club, "Is President Obama Abusing Executive Power?" *U.S. News & World Report,* (undated), http://www.usnews.com/debate-club/is-president-obama-abusing-executive-power.

74. Stephen Dinan, "Border Agents: DHS has no intention of deporting illegals," *The Washington Times,* (March 21, 2016).

75. Rebecca Kaplan, "Obama: I will use my pen and phone to take on Congress," *CBS News,* (January 14, 2014), http://www.cbsnews.com/news/obama-i-will-use-my-pen-and-phone-to-take-on-congress/.

76. Mike Falcone and Erin Dooley, "Obama: Americans 'Don't Want Me Just Standing Around Twiddling My Thumbs'" *ABC News,* (August 6, 2014), http://abcnews.go.com/Politics/obama-americans-dont-standing-twiddling-thumbs/story?id=24871299.

77. Dino Laudati, "The Founding Fathers Wouldn't Recognize US," *News Max Media,* (August 7, 2012).

78. John Adams, *A Dissertation on the Canon and Feudal Law,* (1765).

79. Theodore Roosevelt (1908) quoted in "Beyond Rhetoric: The Demands of Citizenship,) *Los Angeles Times,* (October 21, 2001).

80. Abraham Lincoln (1860), "Abraham Lincoln Papers at the Library of Congress," (accessed March 2016), http://www.loc.gov/teachers/classroommaterials/connections/abraham-lincoln-papers/history3.html.

81. Andrew Jackson, "Quoted in Robert V. Remini, *Andrew Jackson: The Course of American Freedom, 1822-1832,*" (Baltimore: Johns Hopkins University Press, 1981).

82. James Madison, "The Structure of the Government Must Furnish the Proper Checks and Balances Between the Different Departments" (Federalist #51), *Independent Journal*, (February 6, 1788), http://www.constitution.org/fed/federa51.htm.

83. James Madison, "Separation of Powers" (Federalist #47), (January 30, 1788), http://press-pubs.uchicago.edu/founders/documents/v1ch10s14.html.

84. Charles Krauthammer, "The three-cornered fight for the soul of the GOP, " *The Washington Post*, (January 28, 2016), https://www.washingtonpost.com/opinions/the-three-cornered-fight-for-the-soul-of-the-gop/2016/01/28/3188cdca-c5f6-11e5-8965-0607e0e265ce_story.html.

85. Frederic Bastiat, "The State," *Journal des débats*, (1848).

86. Roger Henderson, "Kuyper's Inch," *Pro Rege*, (Volume 36: No. 3, 2008), http://digitalcollections.dordt.edu/cgi/viewcontent.cgi?article=1380&context=pro_rege.

87. Michael Tanner, "Is Socialism Making a Comeback?" *National Review*, (February 10, 2016), http://www.nationalreview.com/article/431071/socialism-v-free-market-capitalism.

88. Tom Schaller, "Gingrich Slams Paulson, Obama, Sarbannes-Oxley, and even W (a little)," *Five Thirty Eight*, (May 24, 2010).

89. Manon McKinnon, "Defining Deviancy Down, " *The American Spectator*, (June 22, 2011), http://spectator.org/articles/37376/defending-deviancy-down.

90. *Oxford English Dictionary* (December 2015 update), "Socialism," http://www.oed.com/view/Entry/183741?redirectedFrom=socialism#eid (accessed: March 2016).

91. Frederic Bastiat, *The Law*, (New York: Tribeca Books, 2015).

92. W. Paul Cockshott and Allin Cottrell, *Towards a New Socialism*, (Nottingham: Spokesman, Betrand Russell House, 1993), http://ricardo.ecn.wfu.edu/~cottrell/socialism_book/new_socialism.pdf.

93. *Wikipedia: The Free Encyclopedia*, "Wikipedia: About," https://en.wikipedia.org/wiki/Wikipedia:About (accessed March 2016).

94. *Wikipedia: The Free Encyclopedia*, "Socialism," https://en.wikipedia.org/wiki/Socialism (accessed March 2016).

95. As an aside, we can speculate, based upon the spelling of the word "characterised" (with an "s" instead of a "z"), that this *Wikipedia* definition was sourced (at least in part) from the United Kingdom, where socialism has older and deeper roots.

96. While generally attributed to Goebbels, its origin may be in Adolf Hitler's 1925 book *Mein Kampf* (Volume 1; Chapter 10), translated by James Murphy.

97. *Wikipedia, the free encyclopedia*, "Leviathian by Thomas Hobbes," (accessed March 2016), https://en.wikipedia.org/wiki/Leviathan_(book) .

98. R. J. Rummel, *Death By Government* (New Brunswick: Transaction Publishers, 1994), Chapter 2.

99. The Library of Congress, "Revelations from the Russian Archives: Ukrainian Famine," (March 2016), https://www.loc.gov/exhibits/archives/ukra.html.

100. R. J. Rummel, *Death By Government* (New Brunswick: Transaction Publishers, 1994), Table 1.2: Twentieth Century Democide.

101. Jeffrey A. Sluka, *Death Squad: The Anthropology of State Terror*, (Philadelphia: University of Pennsylvania Press, 2000).

102. Bernie Sanders, an avowed socialist and Democrat candidate for president, had the support of 84 percent of voters age 17 to 30 in entrance polls conducted before the 2016 Iowa Caucus. Source: "The youth vote has limits." *Time Magazine,* (February 15, 2016).

103. Verne Paul Kaub, *Communist-Socialist Propaganda In American Schools,* (Whitefish: Literary Licensing, 2013).

104. *Pew Research Center*, "Little Change in Public's Response to 'Capitalism' and 'Socialism,'" (December 28, 2011), http://www.people-press.org/2011/12/28/little-change-in-publics-response-to-capitalism-socialism/.

105. *YouGov*, "One third of millennials view socialism favorably," (May 11, 2015), https://today.yougov.com/news/2015/05/11/one-third-millennials-like-socialism/.

106. Sam Sanders, "Why Do Young People Like Socialism More Than Older People Do?" *National Public Radio,* (November 23, 2015), http://www.npr.org/2015/11/21/456676215/why-do-young-people-like-socialism-more-than-older-people.

107. Kyle Pomerleau, "How Scandinavian Countries Pay for Their Government Spending," *The Tax Foundation,* (June 10, 2015), http://taxfoundation.org/blog/how-scandinavian-countries-pay-their-government-spending.

108. Colin Chilcoat, "Frustrating Future for North Sea Oil," *Oil Price,* (January 24, 2015), http://oilprice.com/Energy/Crude-Oil/Frustrating-Future-For-North-Sea-Oil.html.

109. Emily Ekins, "Millennials Don't Know What 'Socialism' Means," *Reason,* (July 16, 2014), http://reason.com/poll/2014/07/16/millennials-dont-know-what-socialism-mea.

110. Ibid.

111. Ibid.

112. Charles Krauthammer, "The New Socialism," *The Washington Post,* (December 11, 2009), http://www.washingtonpost.com/wp-dyn/content/article/2009/12/10/AR2009121003163.html.

113. Frederic Bastiat, "The State," *Journal des débats,* (1848).

114. This oft repeated line, attributed to Goebbels, is likely a variant of an article he wrote entitled: "Churchill's Lie Factory." In it Goebbels wrote: "The English follow the principle that when one lies, one should lie big, and stick to it. They keep up their lies, even at the risk of looking ridiculous." Source: Joseph Goebbels, "Aus Churchills Lügenfabrik," *Die Zeit ohne Beispiel,* (January 12, 1941).

115. This quote, while challenged by some as having no origin other than Internet blogs, is a derivation from a Nietzsche quote from his book *Beyond Good and Evil* (1886), in which his Aphorism number 183 reads: "Not that you lied to me but that I no longer believe you has shaken me."

116. D. James Kennedy, "Commentary: Does the Bible Teach Socialism?" *The D. James Kennedy Topical Study Bible,* (Lake Mary: Charisma House Book Group), page 1557.

117. *The Communist Manifesto* (originally: *Manifesto of the Communist Party*) is an 1848 political pamphlet by German philosophers Karl Marx and Friedrich Engels.

118. Bill O'Reilly and Martin Dugard, *Killing Reagan,* (New York: Henry Holt and Company, 2015), footnote at end of Chapter 28.

119. Paul McHugh, "Commentary: Transgender Surgery Isn't the Solution," *The Wall Street Journal,* (June 12, 2014).

120. Debby Herbenick and Aleta Baldwin, "What Each of Facebook's 51 New Gender Options Means," *The Daily Beast,* (February 15, 2014), http://thedailybeast.com.

121. Opinion Pages: Transgender Today, "Profile of Nick Meinzer," *The New York Times*, (accessed March 2016), http://www.nytimes.com/interactive/projects/storywall/transgender-today/stories/nick-meinzer.

122. "Fifty-eight gender options not enough? Facebook now allows unlimited custom identities," *TV Novosti*, (February 27, 2015), https://www.rt.com/usa/236283-facebook-gender-custom-choice/.

123. Debby Herbenick and Aleta Baldwin, "What Each of Facebook's 51 New Gender Options Means," *The Daily Beast*, (February 15, 2014), http://thedailybeast.com.

124. Opinion Pages: Transgender Today, "Profile of Rhonda Williams," *The New York Times*, (accessed March 2016), http://www.nytimes.com/interactive/projects/storywall/transgender-today/stories/rhonda-williams.

125. Kelsey Harkness, "Minnesota Kindergarten Students Forced to Confront Gender Identity," *The Daily Signal*, (February 29, 2016), http://dailysignal.com/2016/02/29/kindergarten-students- forced-to-confront-gender-identity/.

126. Ibid.

127. Austin Ruse, "College of Pediatricians Calls Transgender Ideology 'Child Abuse,'" *Breitbart*, (March 21, 2016), http://www.breitbart.com/big-overnment/2016/03/21/college-of-pediatricians-calls-transgender-ideology-child-abuse/.

128. S. *Bear Bergman*, "I Have Come to Indoctrinate Your Children Into My LGBTQ Agenda (And I'm Not a Bit Sorry)," *Huffington Post*, (March 7, 2015), http://www.huffingtonpost.com/s-bear-bergman/i-have-come-to-indoctrinate-your-children-lgtbq_b_6795152.html.

129. David Kyle Foster, *Love Hunger: A Harrowing Journey from Sexual Addiction to True Fulfillment*, (Grand Rapids: Baker Publishing, 2014).

130. Ginny Mooney, "Os Guinness Calls for a New Christian Renaissance," *The Christian Post*, (June 18, 2011), http://www.christianpost.com/news/os-guinness-calls-for-a-new-christian-renaissance-51309/.

131. For more than a century, a less-than-confident consensus has agreed to accept that about 620,000 Americans died in the conflict, with more than half of those dying off the battlefield from disease or festering wounds. That was until historian J. David Hacker published a paper that used demographic methods and sophisticated statistical software to study newly digitized US census records from 1850 to 1880. Prof. Hacker's findings, published in the December 2011 issue of *Civil War History*, have been endorsed by some of the leading historians of the conflict. **Source:** "Who, What, Why: How many soldiers died in the US Civil War?" (April 2012), http://www.bbc.com/news/magazine-17604991.

132. Abraham Lincoln, "Second Inaugural Address," (March 4, 1865), The Avalon Project, *Yale Law School*, http://avalon.law.yale. edu/19th_century/lincoln2.asp.